At the age of seventeen, Maren Greve Enthoven left Denmark to go to university in Scotland.

On a brief visit to London, a photographer friend named Ray Harwood took her to Lucy Clayton, a famous modelling agency, and she was immediately offered a Vogue contract by the then editor, Bee Miller, who took her under her wing.

She didn't return to university, but began a career as a top model and was one of the modelling world's best-known faces during the sixties and early seventies.

Her work took her to New York, Paris, Milan and Rome from her base in London.

She is the first to admit that she couldn't so much as boil an egg when she first left home and her teenage years in London without parental help were difficult ones.

She has a son and a daughter of her own and three gorgeous grandchildren.

When her own children (Tania and Peter) left home, Maren had the idea to write this book, in the hopes that she could make the transition to independence just that little bit easier for the many young people stepping out into the world on their own for the first time.

This book was first written for my children, Peter and Tania, and is now dedicated to my grandchildren, Mia, Loulou Rose and Loki.

Maren Greve Enthoven

FROM HOME TO HOME

All You Need to Know When You First Leave Home

AUSTIN MACAULEY PUBLISHERS™

LONDON * CAMBRIDGE * NEW YORK * SHARJAH

ISBN 9781398403970 (Paperback)
ISBN 9781398403987 (Hardback)
ISBN 9781398403994 (ePub e-book)

www.austinmacauley.com

First Published 2021
Austin Macauley Publishers Ltd®
1 Canada Square
Canary Wharf
London
E14 5AA

I also want to say a very big, heartfelt thank you to the NHS for all the amazing work that you do.

A huge thank you to Jessica Nash for helping complete this book, and my granddaughter Mia for always helping me when I needed assistance.

Table of Contents

Introduction

Without my grandma, this book would not have been written as she and my mother gave me all the wisdom, advice and love that I needed when I first set-up home in London.

I had not realised at the time what a fantastic legacy I had inherited and I now, in turn, want to pass on those pearls of wisdom, not only to my children and grandchildren, but also to you. So, this book is for everyone leaving home for the first time.

From Home to Home is a friendly compendium of the advice and information that helped me survive, and enjoy life when I left home.

Setting up on your own for the first time can be a wonderful experience, really exciting. But it can also be challenging when you only have yourself to depend on. This book is written to help make it easy for you to cope and enjoy this new chapter in your life.

'From Home to Home' is essential reading for all young people leaving home and for every parent's peace of mind!

Budgeting.

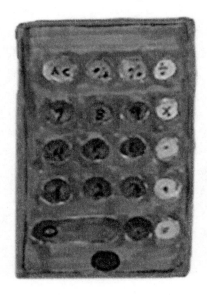

Chapter 1: Budgeting

Aaargh! Budgeting – let's be honest, it may not be the most exciting subject to begin with, but it's certainly one of the most essential.

Through painful experience, I know the importance of getting your budget sorted out from the start.

So here are some thoughts I hope will help you.

First of all, write a list of your monthly and annual outgoings such as rent, utility bills like gas and electricity and council tax etc. And if you have a student loan, this will need to be thought about in the future too. You could save money if you shop around for a good deal on your gas and electricity but you will need to check with your letting agent if it's possible to 'switch'.

Now be honest and include everything: fares, snacks, even that early morning coffee on the way to work or college can easily be forgotten and all add up.

Trust me, you'll soon see what you can and can't afford.

Saving money may seem like an alien concept to you right now, but if you can possibly put a little aside each month, it's a great way to make those extra treats like a weekend away or the wonderful coat that caught your eye the other day, infinitely more possible. You could also buy a second-hand bike which will save you money on travel and keep you fit at the same time. If you're in doubt about any of this, do seek expert advice. You may not enjoy hearing everything they have to say, but knowing you've covered everything will put you in control and give you enormous peace of mind.

There's a great website by Martin Lewis called 'moneysavingexpert.com', which is a good starting point, as well as lots of useful banking apps and accounts that can help with budgeting, such as Starling, Monzo and Chip. A bank manager is also a great source of advice.

There are specially designed bank accounts for people like you who are just starting out alone which can be tailor-made to fit your specific needs. Pop in for a chat and the manager will take you through everything you need to know about working out your budget and running your account well. It's all about 'balancing incomings and outgoings'. Make an effort to build a relationship with your personal contact at the bank. It will put you in good stead in good times and bad.

Talking of bad times, if you should find yourself in deep water don't leave it until it becomes a crisis. The earlier you approach your bank the less painful it will be to fix the problem. Most likely is that you'll have overspent on an overdraft, or have credit card costs spiralling out of control.

If this is the case then banks have customer support units for when things go wrong. The team in these units, depending on your circumstances, could suggest accumulating what you owe into a pot of debt as well as a payment plan to bring you back into the black. They may also check your outgoings so be prepared for some disagreement on what you and they may deem to be necessities.

If despite my reassurances about the support financial experts can give you still feel uncertain, embarrassed or even scared to approach a financial expert, then you can find help online. Sites like 'Which' give great advice and enable you to shop around for the best deals to suit you. There are also very friendly debt management services such as 'StepChange', I know this for a fact as a friend of mine has been helped by them.

Now the budget groundwork is solid and in place the trick is to keep it this way. You need to manage your budget to keep it up-to-date and on track.

So, here's a list of ways you can help keep your finances in order:

1. **Managing your bills:** The easiest way to take the worry out of paying bills and also to save money, is to set up direct debit payments online. Make sure you have enough money in your account to cover these.

2. **Making the most of your savings:** The critical thing here is to shop around. You'll earn more interest if you invest in a long-term account but may not be able to get your hands on your money readily and there may even be penalties for early withdrawals. Take your time to find something that suits you – the right balance between earning interest and accessibility.

3. **Keep receipts safe:** Allocate a drawer or box for all your receipts, guarantees etc. And always try to file your papers properly and quickly, i.e., before they get thrown away! It's easy to check out your rights

online if anything goes wrong – but returning items is made a lot easier if you have those essential pieces of paper at your fingertips.

4. **Keep track of financial changes:** Take a moment every six months or so to revise your breakdown. Especially if you've changed jobs and are earning a little more, you're likely to see a rosier picture than when you started. There are lots of ways your life may change that will impact on what you spend, how you spend and therefore how you split your monthly budget.

5. **Living on the cheap:** There are some great bargains around, and it can be fun to look out for them, so keep your eyes peeled. For example, second hand clothes, call them 'vintage' if you like (!) are really in and there are shops everywhere. It's always such fun to find something unexpected.

Budgeting – The Golden Rules

1. Jot down every expense large or small.

2. Always over rather than under-estimate (bills have a funny habit of always being higher than you'd hoped).

3. Please, please be honest and realistic. If you know you really can't resist the odd taxi, then allow for this.

4. If you find yourself in trouble, don't be an ostrich. Don't be afraid to get advice from an expert – sooner rather than later – they are there to help you.

Now, I'll be honest with you, I certainly wasn't perfect. But with some advice from my father, plus a heavy dose of hindsight, I can now give you these suggestions to help keep you on the financial straight and narrow.

SETTING UP HOME

TO RENT

Chapter 2: Setting Up Home

Finding somewhere to live:

Now you've worked out your budget and know what you can afford for rent, it's time to find the right place for you to live.

When I left University in Scotland at 18, I came to London and had to set up home.

I had very little money, had visited London once or twice but didn't really know it.

To be honest, I was excited but slightly overwhelmed.

An early discovery was Peter Jones, the department store in Sloane Square, which was like a treasure trove where I found so many wonderful and cosy things I wanted to buy.

But first of all, I needed to find a home…

So the first thing I did was to buy myself a music system…well everyone has their priorities!

Seriously though, maybe you're looking with friends for a house to share, or simply a room to rent. Maybe you're looking to lodge with a family or go into your university or college's houses of residence.

Whatever your situation and choice, finding somewhere to live can seem a daunting task, especially if you're moving far from home.

The fact is that setting up home, alone or sharing, should be fun and exciting.

And it can be, but there are certain things that are vital to know and do.

I suggest you make yourself a cup of tea, sit down with a pen and paper, and do some research on the internet of the areas you think you may like to live. Be sure to give yourself plenty of time to do things really thoroughly. It's so important to be in a place where you feel safe and comfortable.

As well as finding properties and rooms online, you can choose to go to a letting agent, but you should check out whether they'll charge you a search fee.

Many do. Never make an arrangement to meet a 'prospective property owner' on your own – always bring a friend.

You need to truly understand what's going to work for you. In short, you need to prepare and make a list of your needs and priorities. I've prepared a checklist but want to emphasise that the most important criteria have to be location and lifestyle.

It makes sense when you think about it. You want to feel comfortable and safe about where you live and your lifestyle has a real impact on where you'll be happiest living. For example, if you take public transport, often work late or go out in town, then having somewhere that's close to the bus and transport networks is a must.

So, get to know the area you plan to live in. It may even be an idea to take a friend and go for lunch. Walk around, go into shops, ask questions. Get an idea of the area and how you feel about it.

With location and lifestyle uppermost in your mind, make your checklist. And as with your budget, I urge you to be ultra-honest with yourself.

An Example Checklist:

- Location – Try not to limit yourself too much if possible. It's interesting to compare and contrast properties, especially in terms of the space you'll get for your money in differing locations.
- Set out your maximum price. Bear in mind that most property owners will require a four to six-week deposit, or even perhaps two months. You will also need to give them confirmation of your income with bank statements and a personal reference. Depending on the market you may be able to negotiate prices down and so seeing slightly more expensive properties may be worthwhile.
- When do you need to move in?
- How long do you want to stay – are you looking for a short-term or long-term let?
- Are you looking for furnished, unfurnished, or partly furnished?
- Are you looking alone, or are a group of you seeking to share, if so, how many? Just a quick word on this – be one hundred percent certain about who you're sharing with. If not close friends, spend time with them before you make a final decision to share. Because sharing space, bills,

chores and kitchen cupboards isn't easy even with people you know well!

- How many bedrooms are needed?
- What are your transport requirements?
- What won't you compromise on?
- Make sure there is a 'deposit protection scheme' – DPS – depositprotecti on.com

Now you're well-equipped to get down to business.

Working with a Letting Agent: A quick look in the paper or online will find you letting agents in your area. Why not make appointments with a couple of them and their lettings team to be sure you're getting the very best service – and deal?

It's important to invest time in building a good relationship with your letting agent. OK, so ultimately, they're working for the property owner, but if your agent understands your needs, they will help you find the right place at the right price.

Be honest. Agents need facts upfront so they can negotiate well and also do some of your own probing. Be sure your agent knows the property owner well so ask away, e.g.:

- Where does the property owner live, especially if abroad – and how are they going to manage the property in the UK?
- Is there an itinerary of items belonging to the property?
- Once you are renting what is the process for getting any items mended/replaced, should they break?
- Are pets allowed?

It's a good idea to see a selection of properties so you can compare and contrast. Your agent has your maximum budget in mind but may be keen to show you something a little above this – which can all be very tempting, but disastrous if you really can't afford it. So do tell your agent upfront if being shown places that break the set budget is a complete no-go.

Take along a friend when you view for the first time. As well as for obvious safety reasons it can be a good idea to have a second opinion, and importantly a second pair of eyes. It's funny how things like checking whether there's enough wardrobe space can be overlooked in the excitement of thinking you've found your first home.

I nearly fell into this trap when I was looking for somewhere to live. Having fallen in love with a delightful place, tiny but cosy, I was utterly blind to the fact that not only were there no drawers or a wardrobe for my ever-burgeoning array of clothes, but there was also no space for any of these things. Had it not been for a chat with my mother and a much-needed reality check, I'd have moved in and regretted it.

There may be some changes you want to make: repaint your bedroom, put up new blinds, hang some pictures on the wall here and there.

Many property owners don't mind these requests as long as they're agreed at the start. It can get very sticky if you start asking for things after the contract has been signed and sealed.

I just can't emphasise enough – ask, ask, ask…

When I was writing this book, I talked with an estate agent who passed on their 'Top Tips' for letting a property, which I'm now delighted to pass on to you.

Top Tips:

Where to begin?

1. **The first step is to contact your local lettings office who will register your details and discuss your search requirements.**

   Think about your desired property type and location. It might be useful to refer to a 'Local know-how' guide (many letting agents have them) if you are unsure on location, or discuss it with your agent who can then help you refine your search.

   - Consider your 'must have' criteria
   - Budget – how much would you be prepared to pay for the right property?
   - Length of tenancy?
   - When do you want to move? We recommend beginning your search around 6-8 weeks prior to your ideal move date.

- Would you like the agent to professionally manage your property during your tenancy?

2. View a selection of properties

Your agent will show you the best properties available in line with your requirements. The London property market for example moves very quickly. It all depends on what part of the country you are going to live. If you find the perfect property, one that suits the majority of your requirements, you may wish to place an offer on the same day – be prepared, it may be the first one you see!

3. Found the right place...Placing an offer

Upon finding a suitable property, complete an offer form with your agent, ensuring all your requirements are clearly stated.
An administration fee is payable at this stage. This amount is fully refundable or transferable should your offer not be accepted.

4. Offer accepted

Upon acceptance of your offer, you will be sent the Tenancy Agreement and other necessary documentation which should be read through thoroughly. Your agent will be pleased to help should you have any questions.

Reference checks will be made at this stage – please ensure you can provide bank details and the contact details of a property owner you may have previously rented from, along with those of your employer.

You will also be issued with a statement of account for your initial payment.

This will include:

- Rent for the first month
- Deposit – equivalent to six weeks rent (make sure your deposit is protected – DPS –depositprotection.com).
- Charge for checking the inventory at the commencement of the tenancy. (The landlord is responsible for the payment of checking-out the inventory when the tenant leaves.)
- Any referencing agency charges.
- Future payments for monthly rent are usually taken in advance by direct debit or standing order so please have your bank account details available to complete the form. Please note the signature must be an original as copies are not accepted by the banks.

5. Moving in

- Provided that all payments, documents and references are in order, your keys will be available for collection on the start date of the tenancy, usually from the office or via an appointment with an inventory clerk. (make sure that this is organised at a convenient time for both of you!).
- You will need to inform your utility providers that you have moved into the property and ensure that all accounts are transferred into your name as quickly as possible.
- A copy of the inventory check-in report will be sent to you (usually by email) shortly after move-in. Should you have any comments or questions, they should be raised as soon as possible after this has been received.

6. What if I need help during my tenancy?

- If your property is managed by your agent, most likely you will be advised of the name and contact details of your property manager (the person who is responsible for looking after the property whilst you are in it). At the start of the tenancy, you should feel free to contact them at any time to discuss any questions or problems you may have.

- If your property is managed by the property owner, you should contact them directly for any maintenance issues. For any questions regarding tenancy agreements, break clauses, payments or renewals, please contact the Tenancy Management Department and they will provide you with all the necessary contact numbers upon moving in.
- If you are still unsure, your property manager will be happy to provide further advice.
- If a break clause is added to your lease, it effectively means that either party has the right to end the lease early if conditions are met. More information can be found at online.

7. **Short let properties – How does a short-term differ from a long-term let?**

- A short-term tenancy is for a term that is less than six months. All monies must be paid in full and in advance (including a 4-6-week deposit).
- Sometimes utility bills are included in the rental amount, with the exception of telephone and broadband fees, payment of which will be detailed in your tenancy agreement.

8. **Moving into Halls of Residence**

When you have been accepted at a college or university, you will be sent a comprehensive pack which details how to go about moving into Halls of Residence and registered local lodgings. As with any hunt for a place to live, I strongly recommend you take time to check out the immediate area to be sure it is the best place for you.

Home Sweet Home

Once you've found the right place for you, the fun can really start. It's time to turn bricks and mortar into 'Home Sweet Home'!

I come from a long line of home-makers. Both my grandma and mother put so much love and care into making wonderfully happy homes.

This, I now realise, whether it be subconsciously or otherwise, had a huge impact on me as I've always tried to create the cosiest home I possibly could.

I found that just a few things can make a big difference; and it really needn't break the bank.

In my case, my music system (of course!), a few cushions, candles and flowers did it for me.

Obviously, everyone is different and you'll know yourself what makes you feel comfortable.

It's those personal touches that count, give you enormous pleasure and say, "This is *my* home."

Here are some other thoughts:

It's lovely to be surrounded by the people you care about (family and friends) and it's so easy to create a montage of your favourite photos. An instant reminder of happy times and nothing could be more personal.

Why not transform and update that boring old sofa with a throw? There's no need to buy a specially made one, instead just visit sales and pick up remnants. Mix and match until you've created a look you love.

Inherited a vile carpet? If you can't afford a replacement, or the property owner won't let you, don't worry, rugs can hide a multitude of sins and are so cosy for bare feet.

I love art and in my setting up home days used to buy prints and posters.

Whenever I could I'd visit art fairs where you can still pick up original pieces, artwork and sculptures by young artists for a relative snip. And who knows, if you choose well, they may turn out to be a great investment.

Often just one statement piece will do the trick, bring a room alive and put a very individual stamp on your home.

And you know nothing instantly freshens up a room more than flowers and luckily many shops and supermarkets offer good quality but cheap fresh flowers and plants. You can also seek out a local florist who may be clearing out flowers that are, only a little, past their best.

If all that water changing, cutting stems and general flower and plant upkeep doesn't do it for you, then the longer-lasting and in the long run potentially cheaper option is 'going fake'. Fake flowers have come a long way. Choose well, and as long as no touching goes on, no-one will notice the difference!

Worried about the initial cost? Don't be. Take a look online, there are some great offers around.

Why not grow your own? No garden? Not a problem. Window sills are just perfect for growing whatever you fancy. Little tubs of herbs can look pretty as well as providing perfect, tasty ingredients. Succulents are also a great option as need little care and attention – just make sure you have 'succulent soil' if they need repotting.

Now, let's talk size. It does matter…

Room a bit on the small side? If so, then here are some suggestions for maximising the space you have.

You'll need a table to eat at every day. Eating off your lap really isn't a long-term option – and bad for the digestion anyway. A small desk or table where you can study, work or eat will always be useful.

And don't forget, if you're really pushed for space be sure that your sofa is a sofa-bed. They're the perfect two-in-one solution for you and any overnight stays.

Now for some trickery. Mirrors are fantastic at creating the illusion of space. Second-hand shops make ideal hunting grounds for bargains. Don't worry about dodgy looking frames, a lick of paint often solves this and as for flaws, well will anyone really notice?

If you have the property owner's permission, then it may be time to start wielding a paint brush around. There's nothing better than a lick of paint to freshen up and make a place your own. Choose light colours and your room will instantly look bigger, while warm tones will give a cosy feel. Why not release your inner Jackson Pollock, go wild and enjoy a result that is uniquely 'you'.

These are just some initial thoughts but there's so much more to creating your first home. This is your first real chance to escape from parental tastes, judgements and restrictions. So go for it. Find your own style. Unsure? Then I suggest you look in magazines and you'll soon find something that you feel says 'that's me'.

If the minimalist look is your style, then a trip to Ikea is probably for you. Their Scandinavian heritage means they're bound to have exactly what you're looking for. However, if a more Gothic or Bohemian look is what you're after, then nothing beats a good old rummage around markets and second-hand shops. With a bit of patience, you're bound to find some treasures you'll love and can afford.

Getting down to the practical items:

If you can afford it, invest in a bed. Your bed is so personal that it's always best to have your own if at all possible. Just have a think about how many other people could have slept on that mattress in your new flat!

I started off with just a new mattress on the floor. In an ideal world, it would have been best to have a bedframe, but at least I knew it was new, clean and importantly, one-owner-only…me. But if you can't afford a proper mattress or frame, then you can buy a decent blow-up bed.

At the very least, you'll need a duvet, blankets and mattress cover, two or three pillows, plus bed linen like a duvet and pillow covers, sheets plus large and small towels.

Also essential are a cooker, fridge, washer/dryer and hoover. And if you need to look smart for work then you will need an iron and ironing board.

If you can't live without a TV, then don't forget the licence. Just one licence per household, not per set. You can also sign up to Netflix or Amazon Prime. A TV wasn't essential for me at all, unlike having music, which was.

Cleaning:

I was horrified to see that people would use a mop which is a handle with lots of cotton strings to clean the floor, surely a proper floor cloth that you can put into the washing machine and get it properly washed and rid of dirt and bacteria, is the only way to clean a floor.

Also, when you have used your different cloths, i.e., kitchen surfaces, dusting, windows, yes also the loo, of course, can you imagine the germs that they carry, so all cloths must be put into the washing machine, after each is used, and on a high temperature.

For the kitchen:

We all have different lifestyles. I loved having people around for dinner and so had to make sure I had enough of everything.

Here are a few of my 'must haves':

Cutlery, including knives, forks, spoons, bread-knife, wooden spoons, plus a whisk, grater and colander.

Crockery, including plates, mugs, cups, saucers, bowls, glasses.

And don't forget the kettle and a couple of saucepans including a frying pan.

A corkscrew might just come in handy too.

These should set you up nicely.

Things you might not realise you can store in the fridge but can:

- Avocados.
- Nuts.
- Bananas.
- Fresh coffee.

And for the freezer…

I cut my bread into slices, store the sliced bread in the freezer, when you need a slice of bread, take it out and put into your toaster. You will always have a lovely slice of toast.

Top tips for making your place your home:

- Look in magazines for inspiration.
- Find a style that's 'you' and that you love.
- Go hunting for treasures. Remember less, really, is more.

SAFETY iN YOUR HOME

Chapter 3: Safety in the Home

Being safe and feeling safe is top of the list when setting up your own home. A little dust here and there won't harm but an unsafe front door most certainly will.

At first it will seem a little daunting with a million and one things to remember – and all down to you – but, in time, everything will fall into place and just seem like second nature.

I just want you to feel safe and comfortable by making some simple suggestions.

Let's start with the obvious – locks, keys and alarms.

I called one of the lock specialists for advice and this is what they told me:

If it's your own home or rented, you can ring the local police station for advice on security. They will come around, free of charge, and tell you if you need any more locks and bars to be completely secure. They will give the best advice as they are impartial unlike commercial companies who have an obvious vested interest.

If you're a tenant and worried about the level of security you are well within your rights to ask your property owner to fit extra door and window locks. A spyhole and chain on the front door are pretty essential too.

Now keys, the cause of many a nightmare. Always losing them? Well, here's a thought that kills two birds with one stone. When you're at home alone, always put the keys in the lock on the inside, turn to double lock the door (if possible) and leave them there. This way nobody can get in from the outside and you'll always know where to find your keys. However, don't do this if there is a window pane close by the door as it's easy for a burglar to break it and be inside before you know it. Also, if the letterbox is too close to the lock, have a flap fitted on the inside of your letterbox to be extra safe and sound.

Take care not to inadvertently lock flatmates out – it's easily done. You can still double lock on the inside but this time take the keys out and get into the habit of leaving them in the same place so that you always know where to find them.

When you go out, you must double lock. You'd be surprised how easy and quick it is to break in with a piece of plastic and burglars have special tools for special locks. But do be sure you're the last to leave as some doors won't open from the inside once double-locked which could mean that you've trapped your friends by mistake.

Inevitably, you will lose your key or get locked out at some point and so arrange to keep a spare set with a reliable friend or neighbour. Do not leave keys under a stone, flower-pot, dustbin or mat please. Burglars are not that stupid – and if your keys are stolen, always change the lock immediately.

Never, ever mark your keys with anything that can be linked to your home, not even with your name. If you have a full key ring then put a blob of paint on your door key so you can find it quickly in the dark. In fact, try to have the door key in your hand when you arrive home at night to avoid having to stand alone outside fumbling for it. I'll be talking more about safety out and about, but this is worth flagging up more than once.

A brief word on alarms. Most properties will have a burglar alarm system fitted but if yours hasn't, ask for one or get one fitted and make sure you use it!

Less talked about, but equally important, are smoke and carbon monoxide alarms. It is a legal requirement for property owners that you are renting from to ensure your flat is fitted with fully working smoke alarms (one for each room and the hallway) and a carbon monoxide alarm. Death by carbon monoxide leakage from gas appliances, fires and boilers etc. have been increasing, so get a special alarm fitted as it could save your life.

Also, potentially life-saving is knowing where and how to turn your gas, electricity and water supplies off. Make this a priority when you first move in. If in doubt, ask.

So, we've dealt with the safety essentials, but there are still a whole host of potential everyday hazards within the home that can be easily avoided with a little care and attention. So, here I'm afraid is rather a long list of **'Dos and Don'ts'**.

Do:

1. Be sure of where your exits are and make sure they're not blocked.
2. Buy a personal alarm to carry with you while you are out and about…and use it if ever you are in danger!
3. Have appliances serviced regularly. Again, this is the responsibility of the property owner and should be carried out on a yearly basis (at least).
4. Make sure heaters are well away from curtains and furnishings, and that they are out of the way where they can't be knocked over.
5. Be sure to turn off appliances when you've used them, like irons, gas-rings, hair-dryers etc. or are going out – turning off switches, pulling out plugs etc.
6. Store inflammable cleaning fluids carefully making sure things like spray cans are not close to heaters or direct sunlight.
7. Invest in a small fire extinguisher and fire blanket, which I suggest you keep in the kitchen. But a damp cloth or blanket will do the same job.
8. Make sure you have the wiring checked. This doesn't just apply to older properties.

And Don't:

1. Ever go out, even around the corner to buy something, leaving candles burning. And blow them out before you go to bed.
2. Dry your clothes too near to open heaters.
3. Think of transforming your harsh lighting by draping a scarf over the shade. Buy a pink or peach light bulb instead!
4. While cooking, leave a saucepan unattended, especially if it contains oil or fat and be sure its handle is not sticking out. If a chip pan (or overheated grill) does catch fire, turn off the heat but don't move or throw water over it. Instead smother the flames with a damp cloth or fire blanket and leave it until it cools.
5. Remove any utensils from the saucepan or frying pan that you may be using – do not balance them on the edge!
6. Use your hairdryer or any other electrical appliance in the bathroom or anywhere near water.

7. Attempt any electrical DIY other than changing plugs or light bulbs as it can be dangerous.
8. Try to fish out that piece of toast in the toaster with a knife while it's still switched on. Tania's girlfriend Charlotte couldn't get the toast out of the toaster and so she used a knife. Don't. Charlotte had a nasty accident. Use a pair of wooden tongs instead. Make sure you have turned the toaster off before you do this.
9. Don't sit in the bath and use your phone/laptop etc, especially if it is plugged into the electricity socket – you will definitely get electrocuted should your device fall into the water!

And before you go out...

1. Make sure all appliances and taps are turned off – and candles blown out.
2. Doors and windows are locked.
3. Try to keep an outside light on or one inside to deter intruders. Anyway, it's nice for you to come home to a well-lit flat.
4. Don't forget your keys.
5. Set the alarm if you have one.
6. Remember to take your personal safety alarm with you – keep it in your handbag, manbag or pocket.

If, despite these safety checks, a fire breaks out, there are some simple steps you must take.

1. Close the door to the room where the fire is.
2. Get everyone out including yourself. If you're in a flat on a high floor, do not use the lift.
3. Phone the fire brigade.
   If you are cut off by the flames, remember that smoke is deadly and so immediately go to a window, smash it with something like a shoe – NOT your fist – and take in the fresh air.

Keeping yourself safe online:

Please be careful who you share your information with online; what personal details you give, who you talk to and what you say; especially on social media channels. You need to protect yourself and be aware that **once it's 'put out there' it 'stays out there'!**

SAFETY
OUT
AND ABOUT.

Chapter 4: Safety Out and About

Just as my mother worried about me when I left Denmark, I used to worry so much about Tania's safety when she left home to go out into the big, wide world. Strangely, I wasn't as worried about Peter safety-wise, maybe because he was tall and strong. Of course that is not always enough.

To prevent something horrible happening, you really need to be aware and keep your wits about you at all times. Please, please make sure you look after yourself as most people looking on will not want to get involved.

To feel safe out at night, choose well-lit streets and walk in the middle of them (just be sure of course that you are safe from cars). Walking in the middle of the street can give you an extra couple of seconds to escape should someone be hiding in a garden or behind a tree.

Try to read the signs. Of course, not every person approaching you will be intent on doing you harm but BE AWARE. A show of confidence is very important. Walk fast and don't make eye contact. Above all, keep calm. A potentially hazardous situation can often be deflected by calmness, a sense of authority and sometimes even a sense of humour.

If you are going to wear headphones and listen to music on your phone, keep the volume down low so that you are still able to hear what is going on around you. stay present at all times.

Use the 'Find My Friends' app to share with your family and friends so that they know where you are.

Always carry a personal alarm, they are inexpensive and make such a horrendous noise that they stun the potential attacker and alert passers-by to your plight.

However, if you do feel uncomfortable, threatened and unsafe, look for a house or a shop where the lights are on, ring the bell and ask for help. You may feel a little silly doing this but better silly than harmed. It is really important to listen to your instincts – they are always right!

Always have an air of confidence and pretend you know where you're going even if you don't.

Have your door keys ready so you can get inside your place quickly. Also, if you can, try to keep an outside light on or at least one on inside as it will help you find you way inside. Lights tend to deter intruders too.

I want you to feel prepared and safe wherever you are when you're out and about and so here are some other guidelines:

Mobile Phones: When you're out always make sure that your battery is charged as you never know when you might need to make that SOS call.

Handbags/Manbags: Tania's had her handbags stolen twice, once in a club and once from her car. When it happened in the club, her bag was right next to her, virtually on her lap. When she looked down, it was gone. When it happened in her car, she had hidden it under some clothes.

Both times Tania thought that her bag had been safe.

Handbags sadly are always being stolen; from clubs, cafes, cars – you name it. Sometimes, it seems it happens right in front of your eyes, even when you think your bag is safe. A favourite for opportunists is when handbags are left on the floor as you sit on a bar stool. As they're so easy to grab and make a quick getaway. The same applies to sitting in cafes and resting your handbag on a free, nearby chair. Best to err on the side of caution and keep in contact with your bag at all times.

The feeling that someone has your keys, money or phone is horrible.

So here are some tips to prevent that from happening:

BE AWARE!

If you're going to a club dancing, make sure your keys and money are safe in an inside pocket, money-belt or small bag across your shoulder – and I mean across so that it's not so easy to snatch.

And the same applies if you're on the streets at night or in crowded conditions – on trains, tubes, buses or in shops. Thieves will even cut the handles of your shoulder bag in a crowd, so be aware all the time. Also, try to walk on the inside of the pavement with your bag on the inside.

However, if someone does snatch your bag give it to them rather than risk injury. Your personal safety is far more important.

Then call the police immediately on 999 – the more information the police have, the better. Apart from anything else, if you have personal insurance, the company probably won't pay out unless you have reported the incident. If your flat/house keys have been stolen with your handbag, make sure you change the locks on your doors as soon as possible to prevent uninvited guests! You can also go to the crime prevention officer at your local police-station. They are there to help and would welcome your visit.

Drugs and Drinks: With drugs easily available, you really need to have your thinking cap on at all times. You'll be surprised how dangerous so called 'friends' can be. If you're out with a group you don't know so well, keep a few things in mind.

NEVER leave your drink unattended in a bar or a nightclub – it could even be a private party – anyone is capable of slipping pills into other people's drinks, even for a laugh – which has proved fatal.

NEVER take pills or drugs of any kind just because everyone else around you is. Think of the possible consequences. Think for yourself and be aware of the risks!

Just because the people around you seem to be enjoying the drugs doesn't mean that you would or that they really are. Also, remember some people have a natural allergy to certain drugs that they may not be aware of, so if they have not been prescribed by your own doctor, don't take them.

Most people enjoy drinking alcohol, and it's only natural that sometimes you'll feel like letting your hair down. Why not? However, there is a fine line between having a drink and having fun, and overdoing it and turning into a mess – and a danger to yourself.

When you are drunk and out of control, you are more vulnerable because of the influence of alcohol. This means you are also less aware and may have what we call 'Dutch courage' to do or try things that you wouldn't normally do, never mind safely negotiating the way home. Don't ever get into an unlicensed taxi.

Know your limits. Keep count and try to remember to line your stomach with some food to help absorb the alcohol.

If you do get drunk, why not take a video of yourself on your mobile and the next day ask yourself if you like what you see! But do not take any inappropriate photos or films to send out or put up on social media!

Okay, let's assume you've been sensible, but what about others? NEVER get into a car that is being driven by someone over the limit. They may think they're fit to drive, but they won't be. Don't put your life into their hands, you may not get it back.

I was given some wonderful advice by my grandma who told me that if ever I was in that situation to tell the driver I was about to be violently sick. It works every time!

Rape and Sexual Assault: Heaven forbid that this should happen to you but in a rape or sexual assault situation, always, always call the police. This may seem like the last thing in the world you want to do, but the attacker must be tracked down before he/she does it to someone else. The police realise how delicate they have to be when dealing with a rape or sexual assault victim so you'll be in good hands.

They will treat the victim gently and they will be looked after by an officer of their own sex in a private room. Rest assured that everything that is said will be treated in the strictest confidence.

Out Driving: Before you start any journey, especially at night, tell people at your destination your time of leaving, the route and what time you hope to arrive. Keep a torch in the car, a fully charged mobile phone for emergency calls and some spare change in the glove compartment.

If for any reason you are feeling uncomfortable, lock your doors.

Never pick up a hitch-hiker. Even a woman alone may have a male partner hiding nearby. If someone appears to need help, don't try to assist. But stop when it's safe and call the police.

Be aware of other drivers signalling faults on your car. Do not stop but drive on slowly until it's safe to stop and then check yourself. If you feel that you are being followed by another car, do not make eye-contact with him or her. Instead, slow down, pull into the left-hand lane – perhaps they'll get bored and drive on. If they don't get bored and try to keep pace with you, keep your cool. Make sure that all your windows and doors are locked, drive on until you come to a busy well-lit public place like a petrol station, shop, hospital or police-station. In fact wherever there are other people. Take down their registration number and call the police.

If you are out in the country, make sure that where you stop is a well-lit farm or house, then pull up and sound your horn. Put on the hazard lights and flash your lights.

If you have been forced to stop, do not turn off your engine. If the pursuer comes towards you, you must reverse so you can drive away as quickly as possible.

If you have a breakdown, drive on the hard shoulder and call your rescue service on your mobile. If for some reason you don't have the number or don't belong to a rescue service, then you must aim for the nearest emergency telephone (there is a mile between them) where calls are free.

Here are the safety guidelines from the AA:

Breaking down can be dangerous, particularly if you're on a motorway. Here's what you need to do to stay safe before you call us, and while we're on our way.

1. **Make sure you're in a safe place**. Move your vehicle off the road if possible (watch out for any soft verges), or pull up onto the hard shoulder if you're on a motorway and can't turn off at the next exit. Make sure you stop as far to the left as you can, with the wheels turned to the left.

2. **Put your hazard warning lights on**. If it's dark or foggy, keep your sidelights on too.

3. **Stay well away from moving traffic**. It's usually safest to get out of your car (using the doors facing away from passing traffic) and wait behind a barrier. If you're on a motorway, move up the bank if you can.

4. **Leave animals in the car.**

5. **Wear a reflective jacket** if you have one.

6. **Don't put a warning triangle on the hard shoulder** if you're on a motorway – it's not safe. If you're on a road and it's safe, you can put a warning triangle at least 45m (50 yards) behind your vehicle.

7. **Call on 0800 88 77 66** if you need help, or **<u>use the app</u>**. Don't attempt even a simple repair if you're on a motorway.

   If you don't have a mobile, **walk to an emergency phone** on your side of the carriageway. Follow the arrows on the posts at the back of the hard shoulder – the phone is free and connects directly to the police.

Remember that the hard shoulder is only for emergencies, not for making calls, having a stretch or toilet stops.

On a smart motorway?

There's no hard shoulder, so follow these steps instead.

1. **Stop at an emergency refuge area (ERA)**, motorway service area or leave at the next junction.
2. If this isn't possible, try and **get the vehicle off the carriageway**.
3. If you have to stop in a traffic lane, **turn on your hazard lights** as soon as possible.
4. If you're in the left-hand lane, and it's safe to do so, **get out of the vehicle** on the left-hand (passenger) side and **wait behind the barrier**.
5. If you can't get out, or you're in another lane and it's not safe to leave the vehicle, **stay in the car with your seatbelt on and dial 999**.
6. If you stop in an ERA, you must **use the SOS phone** to contact the Regional Control Centre when you stop, and before you leave.

10% of all fatal accidents involve cars parked on the hard shoulder. But just to make you feel a little better, assaults on people on the motorway are extremely rare.

Parking: When parking, look for a place where there are plenty of people, and if it's dark, a road with good lighting. Never leave anything of value in your car. A thief can easily open the car boot. Make sure that you lock your car when leaving – one car theft in five is from an unlocked car.

If you have to use a multi-storey car-park, be very careful. Again choose a space which is well-lit and close to the staircase. If there is an attendant try to park as close as possible to his/her booth.

When you're going out it's useful to have 'rehearsed' in your head the bad things that could happen, so that you can work out your response and be prepared.

But the best piece of advice I can give you is **BE AWARE** at all times and **TRUST YOUR INSTINCTS.**

Chapter 5: How to Make Cleaning Easy

I really had to learn the hard way, so please let me help you so you don't.

Okay, let's put the record straight. I'm not ever going to convince you that cleaning is about to become a favourite pastime or the most fun you'll ever have. In fact, it can be pretty boring. Why spend time cleaning our homes when there are much more exciting things to do?

I read in a newspaper that very few people spring clean their homes, but I'm sorry to have to tell you it is absolutely essential. The fact is that we need to live in a clean home for both our health and happiness.

So let's make it as easy as possible.

Of course, a great solution is to have a cleaner and if you're sharing, you may all agree it's worth chipping in to pay for one. But I'm going to assume this isn't an option and so want to make things nice and simple.

You'll be amazed at what you can do in just an hour and there's so much to be gained. Not only will you feel free to invite people to pop in but a clean home gives you a good feeling inside and a real sense of achievement.

In fact, why not turn your cleaning session into a workout? All that hoovering, dusting, mopping and climbing stairs is great for toning up and building stamina.

So, pop on the marigolds and the music, get fit and get cleaning...

The Golden Rules

Be organised: If you share make a list of chores and agree a rota. For example, who and when empties the dustbins, cleans them and puts them outside. Put the list up where everyone can see it and make sure everyone sticks to it. It's in everyone's interest to play fair as there are other people's feelings to consider and especially after a busy day, it's very important to come home to a pleasant atmosphere.

Keep a pad handy and write down when something needs fixing or replacing, such as light-bulbs, and fit these tasks in, when you have the time.

Try not to do any cleaning at the weekend or on your day off. You've simply got to have days when cleaning does not encroach on your time. Of course, if you have the time to do everything in one day, great, but most likely school, college or your job will mean you don't and so a little each day may well be the way to crack it – and less boring. Up to you.

Spring clean: Essential – as I've already said. Look online for great deals for a professional spring clean if you can afford it, or otherwise get set for an intense session at least twice a year. The trick is not to let your house become too dirty.

Clean outside your front door: If there's not dirt outside you can't bring it inside.

Kitchens and bathrooms are a priority: In particular loos and baths must be kept clean – always.

Always use clean cloths and mops: Pop mop heads and cloths into the washing machine, or at the very least rinse with bleach to rid them of germs and dirt.

Take care of appliances: Be sure to read and keep instruction manuals – this is VERY important.

Turn off electrical appliances before cleaning them: Open all doors and windows (if it's not raining, of course) put on some music and start cleaning. Now some help with specific chores.

Making light of laundry: One of the biggest blows you'll have when you first start to live away is the discovery that the magic laundry basket you had at home cannot be found anywhere else.

You know the one – it had the ability to take dirty clothes and miraculously transform them into clean, ironed and folded clothes that suddenly appeared in your drawer.

Well, the reality is you'll never find another laundry basket like this in the world, now you have to do the laundry yourself, so here goes.

Your friend – the washing machine. Treat this machine with respect and it will treat you well in return. Read the instruction book carefully. Read labels, never overload and if you're in doubt about the material, always choose the lowest setting. Turn jeans inside out, empty pockets, put delicates like bras and tights in a pillowcase or laundry net bag for extra protection and be sure to separate whites and coloureds and hand wash items. A good idea is to use fabric softener – it makes ironing easier – and limescale protection products like Calgon tablets.

Bear in mind that clothes and sheets are so much easier to iron when they aren't absolutely bone dry. And when tackling a shirt, do the collar and cuffs first, then the sleeves and attack the body of the shirt last – concentrating on the front panel which is what people notice!

As with washing, if you're not sure of the material set the iron on the lowest heat or a good idea is to do a test somewhere inside and where no one can see if things do go wrong.

Finally, try not to let washing and ironing build up, it lessens the pain. Remember to turn the iron off when you have finished and put in a safe place to cool down.

The joys of hoovering: In Denmark, it is a mark of respect to take your shoes off when visiting people in their homes as it is considered an honour to be invited in. So, it's a good habit to get into because you don't bring any dirt into the house – just make sure you don't have any holes in your socks, mind you, you're just as welcome with holes!

Anyway, back to hoovering. Read the instructions carefully, be sure to use a clean air filter and if your hoover has bags that need changing, do so regularly for the most effective, fastest results. It's usually best to hoover after you've dusted for obvious reasons and do move furniture about as you'll be surprised what can lurk beneath, like crumbs and coins. Also worth remembering is that hoovers do more than floors, they also do a mean job on sofas, chairs and even curtains. Mind you, take care if your curtains are very old or precariously hung.

Smear-free windows: Dirty windows, especially if you live in a city, can be quite a challenge. However, there's something quite depressing about peering through murky glass, so just think of those toned-up arms at the end of it and get down to business.

Draw back any curtains or blinds and start by washing down the woodwork. Then arm yourself with either a clean soft cloth or chamois leather, some Windolene or warm water and off you go. If you can't get hold of Windolene and the state of your windows demands more than just warm water, then white vinegar with water is a terrific alternative. Be warned, whatever you use, there's a lot of rubbing involved for a perfectly smear free zone. Oh joy!

Of course, all these suggestions work equally well on interior glass and mirrors.

Fantastic floors: The fact is, all floors need looking after. They should be swept or hoovered (yes, hoovering is a brilliant, quick, effective alternative to sweeping) regularly to stop the build-up of dirt which makes them a lot easier to clean and polish.

Depending on whether your floors are wood, cork, linoleum, terracotta or ceramic tiles, you'll need to use different cleaning products. Don't worry though, the solutions are cheap and easy to find. For example, for ceramic, terracotta and marble tiles, use hot water and synthetic detergents such as Ariel/Flash or a similar cleaner works well on linoleum and cork. For vinyl, wood and painted floors, use detergent or pure soap remembering to rinse well with clean, warm water.

Dynamic dusting: Flicking a feather duster around may look the part but it's worse than useless as it simply scatters the dust to another destination. To do the job properly, you'll need a damp cloth to wipe over surfaces – remembering to clear surfaces first and lift items (!) – and get right into dirty corners. If you have books, then dust those with a dry cloth, taking care to place these back on a dry surface afterwards. If you spot cobwebs that are out of reach, pop a duster on a household broom and job done.

A spotless bathroom...and loo: Constantly used, constantly becoming dirty; loos and baths need intense cleaning and an eye kept on them at all times.

You can clean the bath, sink, shower (and bidet if you have one) using Flash or Cif and a clean cloth or sponge. Because these items do become grotty very quickly, it's an idea to keep the cleaning kit to hand and install a 'clean up after you've used' rule.

Loos need scrubbing with good strong bleach which should be left in the bowl for as long as possible before flushing.

And don't put anything except loo paper into the loo!

Limescale often builds up around taps and in particular on showers heads which means you won't get that hit of water we all love. Limelite will immediately lift the limescale or you can use bicarbonate of soda with a little water for the same result.

Shower curtains left without care and attention can become very unpleasant with outbreaks of mildew. The trick is to keep the curtain clean and not to draw it back after use, but if the horse has bolted and you already have mildew then either replace or scrub down with a mild solution of bleach and water. You can also get more environmentally friendly products to use instead.

And you'll need to wipe down all the surfaces including doors and floors and clean mirrors bearing in mind the hints made earlier in this section.

The fact is that often bathrooms and loos harbour unpleasant smells and bacteria. There are some lovely, natural room sprays around, but a simple solution is to light a match and you will see that almost instantly any nasty smells have gone.

A beautiful bedroom: For me, my bed is my ultimate haven.

Your bedroom should be a place of calm and freshness not just to encourage a good night's sleep but also to create a beautiful 'me space' to relax in at any time. To keep it this way just takes a little effort.

Your bed needs some TLC on a regular basis so start by airing it as often as possible. Try to turn the mattress when you can at least and give it a good hoover. It is really good to invest in anti-allergy mattress protector to keep it clean. If you have a duvet it's nice to hang it over a chair next to an open window when it's time to change the bedding or if you are lucky enough to have a garden, you can hang it outside. Give blankets the same treatment.

You'll be amazed how dusty the insides of wardrobes and drawers can become and so wipe them down with Flash (or an environmentally friendly alternative) and keep carpets and surfaces clean with weekly dusting and vacuuming.

Now your wardrobe and drawer space are spotless, please make sure that the clothes that go back in are also spotless.

Also a good idea is to pop in a bar of lavender soap to keep moths at bay. That's the hard work done.

And finally...the kitchen: It makes sense to clean the kitchen last of all if you're doing a day's blitz. You've got to be able to make yourself cups of tea and coffee, break for lunch, change your water etc and having one untidy place seems to make sense. I think you know what I mean.

Kitchens can be tricky as you really do need to pull all appliances away from the wall. You'll need to empty cupboards quite regularly as products can seep out of packs and jars. Also it's important to keep an eye on sell by dates. Get rid of any food which is out of date.

I've already covered cleaning floors and surfaces and so we're going to focus on those kitchen specific items that will need your attention.

The fridge and freezer: Empty the fridge, taking care to throw out any food that's out of date. You can then either use a supermarket bought fridge cleaner or else a solution of bicarbonate of soda and water will work.

You may be in luck and have a self-defrosting freezer. If not, then here goes. When tackling the freezer, you can preserve the food stored there if you pop it into a clean, dry kitchen sink and cover it completely with newspaper. The newspaper will keep the food frozen. Then using a wooden spoon, loosen and scrape off the ice that's accumulated and clean it very quickly. You can also put some newspaper on the floor with a tea towel on top to catch any falling ice.

You'll probably need to defrost once every two months unless of course your fridge self-defrosts.

If your fridge has an unpleasant odour despite this clean then leave half a lemon in there to take the smell away.

Cookers: Whether you have a gas or electric cooker; the hob and the oven will need to be cleaned very regularly. The longer you leave things the tougher it's going to be to clean.

Of course the best thing to do is clean as you go, giving inside and outside surfaces a good wipe with a clean cloth with a cleaning product after every use. Any spillages on hobs should remove easily if attended to at the time. However, if some stains are persistent just cover with salt and wipe a little later. This way you prevent the nasty build-up of grime and grease which make cleaning ovens one of the most dreaded of household chores.

If you have a gas cooker, take off all the burners and soak in the sink. Give the burners and trays a good scrub with a stiff brush and soapy water. Wipe down the top of the grill, top and sides of the cooker with a soft cloth and cleaning product.

If pilot lights have gone off during cleaning, make sure you put them back on.

However, if you have an electric hob, then wipe all the surfaces with a suitable cleaning product unless you have a special surface in which case just look in the instruction book to find the right cleaner to use.

If you would like to use a less toxic cleaning method for the inside of your oven, I suggest you just use a scrubbing brush and any strong detergent, but regular soap will do just as well. Roll up your sleeves, put on your marigolds and get stuck in.

The dishwasher: If you have one, lucky you, but you must take care of it. Read the instructions, don't over stack, use rinse aid and salt and use an intense cleaner every once in a while to keep it in tip-top condition.

The toaster: Probably one of the most used appliances after the kettle and it too needs a little love from time to time. Crumbs collect inside and so turn the toaster off and unplug it. Turn upside down and give it a good shake. You can just wipe the outside with a normal cleaner or soapy water if you prefer.

Some Cleaning Cupboard Musts

Fairy liquid: Dilute for everyday cleaning or use more concentrated to remove stains. Mix with a little bleach for a really fabulous kitchen and bathroom cleaner.

White vinegar: Vinegar is a great all-round cleaner. Mix with warm water for cleaning windows or measure about a cup's worth of vinegar and empty into the drum of your washing machine (keep hold of the cup!). You can also use vinegar in your dishwasher – as above, empty the contents of the cup over the inside of the main body of the washing machine. Vinegar is also great for removing nasty smells from dustbins.

Bicarbonate of soda: Also has many uses and is a natural powder which can be used for cleaning dirt and grime. Just sprinkle onto a wet sponge and off you go!

Bleach: For hardcore germ busting.

Top Tips for Everyday Disasters

Dry cleaning disasters: Here are some tried and tested solutions for when things go wrong:

If the disaster is on something that is 'dry clean only' then do nothing and take it straight to a dry cleaner. Home-made attempts at removal tend to make the dry cleaner's challenge much worse.

Nail varnish spills: Interestingly, nail varnish remover doesn't work on nail varnish spills. Instead dab the spills with concentrated Fairy Liquid.

Red wine spills: Cover the stain with lots of salt, leave and then rinse with cold water.

Paint: If the stain is emulsion, then water will do the trick. If gloss paint has been spilled then you'll need to dab on white spirit.

Coffee: Soak in a biological detergent or treat with a product like Vanish.

Chocolate: Soapy water usually does the trick or you can soak in a biological detergent.

Lipstick and lip-liner: Apply white spirit and watch the stain disappear.

Perfume stains: Just rinse in warm water then wash as normal.

Chewing gum: Scrape off what you can then put the clothing in the freezer for about an hour. If the chewing gum still sticks then try putting the item between two pieces of brown paper and gently iron.

Melted candle wax: Put greaseproof/brown paper over the wax with a tea-towel on top and iron on a low setting – the wax will melt onto the paper.

Grease marks on leather: Rub gently with Fairy Liquid then polish when dry. That's it on cleaning!

Now you should have a clean home and hopefully, a very happy one.

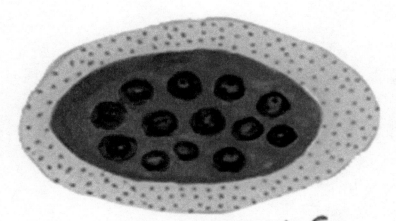

MEAT BALLS

RECIPES.

Chapter 6: Easy Family Recipes

I told Peter and Tania that I couldn't boil an egg when I got married. I am afraid it's true.

I don't want that to happen to you so I have written down some of my children's favourite recipes and made them easy.

Avocado dip

3 avocado pears

Juice of 1 lime

1 sweet green chilli, if not possible, a dash of sweet chilli sauce

1 cup of chopped peeled tomatoes

1 clove crushed garlic

½ onion, very finely chopped

Place tomatoes in a bowl of very hot water, leave for five minutes and the skin should peel off easily. Peel the avocados and remove stones. Cut into small cubes and mash with a fork. Add the juice of the lime (to also stop discolouring as well as add great flavour).

Chop tomatoes and onion very finely and add to avocado, crushed garlic and chilli sauce. Serve in a nice bowl with tortilla chips or crudités.

Avocado dip or 'guacamole'

3 avocados (makes 2 cups)

½ small red onion, finely sliced

1 green sweet chilli

1 tablespoon of flat parsley or coriander

Juice of 1 lime

A little salt and, if you feel like it, garlic (quantity really depends on how much you like garlic with this amount of avocados but I would suggest one large clove.

Peel the avocados, remove the stones, mash the flesh in a bowl or use a stone mortar. Stir in all the ingredients, also tomatoes, if you are using them.

Season with salt.

Crudités to have with the above dips:

Carrots
Cauliflower
Celery
Radishes
Cucumber
Spring onion
Apple

Whatever raw vegetables you like to serve, make sure you wash them well and chop them into easy-to-handle pieces.

Aubergine mozzarella – starter for 4 people

1 large aubergine
2 cloves of crushed garlic
2 cups of wheat crackers
Olive oil

1 tin chopped tomatoes in juice
2 tsp of fresh basil (or ½ tsp dried) 500 grams mozzarella cheese salt and pepper to taste

200°C/400°F/Gas 6 – middle shelf

Wash and cut the aubergines, put into a sieve, lightly salt them, leave for 30 minutes. Rinse and pat dry with kitchen paper.

Heat a little olive oil in a frying pan, fry the aubergines until soft and golden (about five minutes on each side). Drain on kitchen paper to get rid of any excess oil.

Oil an oven dish, pour in the tomatoes with the garlic and basil (salt and pepper to taste), then put on half the aubergines, then half of the sliced mozzarella cheese, add the crushed wheat crackers then the other half of aubergines and lastly the rest of the cheese. Put lid on and place in the oven for 20 minutes. Uncover for the last 5-10 minutes until it's golden on top.

Aioli

An original recipe from a lovely hotel in Venice where I used to eat it on bread instead of butter!

Aioli is used as a dip for crudités, fish soup and any other recipe that requires mayonnaise if you're a garlic lover.

4 egg yolks
Olive oil (about ½ litre)
6 crushed cloves of garlic

First, make the mayonnaise – put the egg yolks into a blender and very, very slowly add olive oil drop by drop until it emulsifies. Then add the garlic. Pour mixture into bowl and put in fridge for one hour.

Basic white sauce (for parsley sauce, cauliflower cheese etc.)
2 cups milk
2 tbsp flour
2 tbsp butter
Salt and pepper to taste

Melt butter slowly in a saucepan. Stir in the flour using a wooden spoon. Over a low heat add the milk slowly and stir constantly until it thickens to the correct consistency. Take off heat and season.

Cheese fondue

1 cup of white wine
2 tbsp kirsch
2 crushed cloves of garlic (optional)
2 cups grated gruyere cheese
2 cups grated Emmental cheese

1 tbsp cornflour
Freshly grated nutmeg
Salt and pepper to taste

Make sure that the fondue pot is safe (regulate the flame very low as it's only to keep the pot warm). Pour the wine into the fondue pot, heat to nearly boiling. Very slowly add the grated cheese to the hot wine, make sure it's melted. Keep it hot. Combine the cornflour with a little kirsch. Stirring all the time, add to the cheese mixture. Add nutmeg, salt and pepper.

Keep the flame low and serve with French bread and salad.
Serves about four.

My vegetarian chilli

4   tbsp olive oil
2   medium chopped onions
3   crushed cloves of garlic

1 green pepper, 1 yellow pepper finely chopped
3 cups of vegetable stock
1 cup tomato paste
2 cups chopped tomatoes

2 cups frozen corn
2 tins red kidney beans
1 tsp chilli powder
2 tsp fresh chopped oregano
1 tsp cumin powder
2 tsp fresh chopped basil
Salt and pepper to taste

Sauté garlic and onion in the oil until transparent (do not let brown). Add everything else and simmer for 55 minutes. For a classic chilli, add one lb of minced beef.
Serve with creme fraiche and a salad.
Serves about six.

Tania's cauliflower cheese

1 cauliflower
1 onion
4 bacon rashers (optional)
2 tbsp butter
1 pint white sauce (page 49)
2 cups grated Cheddar cheese
Salt and pepper to taste

Wash and trim cauliflower. Break it into small pieces and boil for about 15 minutes. Put the cauliflower pieces in a buttered baking dish and keep warm.

Peel and chop the onion. Cut the bacon rashes into small pieces. Fry for 5-6 minutes until the onion is transparent and the bacon is cooked. Sprinkle over the cauliflower.

Make white sauce and add the Cheddar cheese and season. Pour the sauce over the cauliflower and put under a hot grill or until the top is golden and crisp.

Serves about 2-4.

Couscous

You can steam or marinate couscous. If you steam it, pour the water or stock over it and let it stand for about 15 min. If you want to, marinate it, which I feel is the tastiest as the texture has more bite to it.

10 oz couscous
1 red onion
1 red pepper
1 yellow pepper
3 tomatoes
Herbs – parsley, coriander and basil
Salt and pepper to taste.

How to Marinate: Put the amount of couscous you need (about 10 oz for four people) into a bowl with the olive oil and lemon juice (enough for a dressing). You can also use balsamic vinegar or lime juice instead of lemon juice, it really is personal taste. Then put a red onion chopped very finely, a red and yellow

pepper, three chopped tomatoes and a large handful of freshly chopped herbs –
parsley, coriander and basil. Add salt and pepper to taste.

Serves about 2-4.

Danish meatballs with parsley sauce

½ lb minced beef
½ lb minced pork
1 chopped onion
1 grated potato
1 egg
1 crushed clove of garlic
Little oil and butter for the frying pan
White sauce
1 handful of parsley
Salt and pepper to taste

Put all ingredients into a food processor and mix for two minutes.

Form the mixture into small balls (golf ball size). Put the oil and the butter
into a frying pan over a low heat. Put the meatballs into the frying pan and fry
for five minutes on each side.

Serve with parsley sauce and mashed potatoes (white sauce recipe on page
49 – just add parsley).

Serves about 4-6.

Dolls House Cake

2 cups crushed ginger biscuits
2 cups grated chocolate (best quality 72% cocoa solids)
2 cups whipped cream
½ cup honey
½ cup butter

Put the ginger biscuits into a saucepan over a low heat with the butter and
honey. Take off the heat and pour half the mixture into a glass bowl followed by
a layer of chocolate, then the last of the biscuits and another layer of chocolate
and finish with the whipped cream.

Eggs Florentine

1 large packet of frozen spinach

8 tbs double cream

4 eggs

6 tbsp grated Cheddar cheese

Grated fresh nutmeg

Salt and pepper to taste

Put the spinach into a saucepan until thawed, then add the double cream and salt and pepper to taste. Transfer to a greased oven dish and make space for four eggs. Break the eggs into the spaces, sprinkle the grated cheese on top and lastly the fresh nutmeg. Bake for 10-12 minutes in a moderate oven and serve immediately.

Serves two as a main course.

Fish cooked in foil in the oven

Any fish you like (cleaned)

Juice of 1 lemon/lime

Dill or herbs of your choice

Salt and pepper to taste

Olive oil

Put a large double piece of foil on a baking tray (enough to cover the fish). Oil the foil and having put the herbs inside the fish place the fish onto the foil. Pour over the lemon or lime juice and then cover the fish with the foil like a parcel.

Cook for about 20 minutes, medium heat (200°C/400°F/Gas 4) middle shelf.

Always ask the fish-monger to clean the fish. If you have any questions, he/she will always be very helpful. I try to cook fresh fish at least once a week.

My grandmother's chicken

8 large pieces of chicken

225 grams butter (1 pat)

2 cups very finely chopped celeriac root

2 very finely chopped onions

2 very finely chopped carrots

1 handful of parsley

1 sprig of tarragon

3 handfuls of halved seedless grapes

½ pint double cream

1 cup brandy

Salt and pepper to taste

Put the butter in a saucepan to melt and then add the chicken pieces. Cook for 10 minutes and then add the finely chopped vegetables, grapes and herbs. Cook for another 10 minutes. Next add the whisky and cream and cook for yet another 10 minutes.

Serve with mashed potatoes or rice and a salad.

Serves about six.

My oat cookies

180 grams oats

100 grams oat flour

80 grams oat flour or almond flour

200 grams palm or coconut sugar

4 tsp orange or vanilla extract

150 grams melted coconut oil

4 eggs

150 grams chocolate buttons (dark or white chocolate)

1 teaspoon of bicarbonate of soda

A pinch of salt.

Mix all dry ingredients together – if you like more taste of orange you can also grate orange rind.

In another bowl mix together the vanilla or orange extract with the melted coconut oil. Then mix the dry mixture with the liquid mixture. Beat the eggs and slowly stir into the mixture. Finally, add the chocolate. Use your hands to mix it.

Take a dessert spoon and roll into small balls. Place on a baking tray (lined with greaseproof paper). Use the back of a fork to flatten the cookies.

Bake in the oven on 200°C/400°F/Gas 4 for about 12-15 minutes or until golden brown but still soft.

Once ready, leave to cool on a wire tray, they will be firmer when cooled.

Mormor's meatballs

½ pound of minced beef
½ pound of minced pork (if you feel like making meatballs with lamb, that's
  just perfect too)
1 whole onion finely chopped.
3 cloves of garlic, very finely chopped
1 medium sized potato finely grated
A handful of mint, finely chopped
A handful of parsley finely chopped
1 teaspoon of salt (and pepper too if wanted)
1 large egg beaten
Butter and olive oil

Put all ingredients into a bowl and mix together, except the butter and olive oil.

Mix well and leave in fridge for about an hour.

Next put some olive oil and butter into a frying pan. Take the meatball mixture out of the fridge. Take a dessertspoon of the mixture into your hands and roll it into a ball. Fry the meatballs on both sides, making sure they are cooked.

This is dish is lovely served with sweet potatoes, chips or a salad or lots of your favourite vegetables.

Makes around 20 meatballs.

Homemade lemonade

5 lemons or limes (or a mixture)
½ cup brown sugar or honey
2 pints of boiling water

Scrub the lemons or limes and halve them, then squeeze out the juice. Add the juice and sugar (or honey) to the boiling water, pour into a jug, adding the squeezed lemon (or lime) halves. Cover and cool. When ready to serve strain liquid through a sieve and decorate with slices of lime – it's very easy and so tasty!

Hollandaise sauce

120 grams butter
3 large egg yolks
2 tbsp lemon juice
Pinch of salt

Melt the butter in a saucepan. Place eggs, lemon juice and salt in a blender and blend for 15 seconds.

When the butter has melted, let it cool just a little then pour it into blender slowly over the other ingredients and blend.

If you want to keep the sauce warm, keep it in a bowl over hot water, this is called a 'Bain Marie'.

Scrambled eggs

2 or 3 eggs (depending on how hungry you are)
Knob of butter

Beat the eggs in a heatproof bowl (that will sit comfortably in a saucepan of water). Bring a saucepan of water to a simmer and place the bowl with the eggs over the saucepan of water. Add a knob of butter, start mixing with a wooden spoon. You will see after about two minutes, the eggs will start to stick around the edges of the bowl.

Turn of the heat, keep stirring until the eggs become mousse like (around 3-4 minutes). Remember the eggs will keep cooking even of the heat.

Serve warm with toasted sourdough and lots of butter.

Hummus – recipe 01

250g tinned or dried chickpeas (soak dried chickpeas in water overnight)

1 cloves of crushed garlic
2 tbsp of olive oil

Juice of 1 large lemon
3 tbsp of tahini
2 tbsp creme fraiche

A little chopped parsley, to garnish

Drain and rinse chickpeas, cover with water and cook for 1.5 hours until tender. Add the crushed garlic and simmer for 30 minutes with the lid on.

Allow to cool.

Put the olive oil, lemon juice and creme fraiche into a blender. Slowly add the chickpeas with their liquid and garlic. Blend until smooth.

Put into a serving dish, sprinkle with chopped parsley and cool.

Delicious served with pink onions and pitta bread.

Hummus – recipe 02

12 oz tinned or dried chickpeas (soak dried chickpeas in water overnight)

2 cloves of chopped garlic

½ tsp of crushed cumin seeds

1 small red chilli (dried)

2 tablespoons of tahini (sesame paste)

4 tablespoons of cold-pressed virgin olive oil

Lemon juice to taste

Salt and pepper to taste

Drain and rinse the chickpeas and pour into a blender or food processor with the freshly chopped garlic, chilli and tahini until smooth. Add olive oil, lemon juice, salt and pepper to taste.

French Omelette

4 large eggs

½ cup butter

Salt and pepper to taste

Break eggs into a dish and season with salt and pepper. Whisk thoroughly.

Heat the frying pan and put in the butter. As it's foaming, add the beaten eggs.

Lift the edges and make sure all the uncooked mixture runs underneath the cooked eggs. When it is cooked and the bottom is golden, lift the omelette and fold in half.

If you want to make a Spanish omelette add 2 cooked and thinly sliced potatoes, 1 chopped onion and a cup of peas to the egg mixture. You can put in anything you fancy really.

Serves two.

Leg of lamb

3 kg leg of lamb
½ cup butter
½ a finely cut onion
2 cups white wine
A sprig of rosemary
8 cloves of sliced garlic
Salt and pepper to taste

Grease a large baking tin.

Take the lamb and with a small knife make some cuts into the outer layer of skin and insert the garlic. Then rub the meat with the rosemary and pepper.

Put the lamb into the oven at 220°C/410°F/Gas 4 for about half an hour.

In the meantime, sauté the finely cut onions in butter and white wine and pour the entire mixture over the lamb. Take the cheese and the creme fraiche and stir together, pour all over the leg of lamb.

Place into the oven for another hour at 210°C.

Turn the oven off and let it sit for another 20 minutes. Then take out, carve and serve with a salad and/or vegetables of your choice.

Serves six.

My mother's chicken liver pate

12 to 14 cleaned chicken livers
2 medium onions
½ lb of bacon
1 large egg
3 crushed cloves of garlic
2 cups double cream
½ egg cup of juniper berries
½ cup of brandy
½ tsp ground cloves

Salt and pepper to taste

Chop the onions and bacon into small cubes and fry until transparent. Pour into a liquidiser along with the chicken livers and the rest of the ingredients. Pour into a greased flame-proof dish or baking tin and stand in a baking tray of water (Bain Marie) in the oven.

Cook slowly for 2.5 hours at 150°C/300°F/Gas 2.

Wait until completely cooled and seal with melted butter. This dish also freezes very well.

Bran muffins

2 cups whole-wheat flour
2 cups wheat-bran
1.5 tsp baking soda
Rind of 1 orange
Juice of 1 orange
½ cup sultanas
½ cup of crushed almonds or walnuts
2 cups or buttermilk
2 eggs beaten together
1 tbsp of molasses
1 tbsp of honey
½ tsp nutmeg
2 tbsp olive oil
1 tsp of salt

Preheat oven to 170°C/350°F/Gas 3.

Put flour, wheat-bran, salt, soda and nutmeg into a bowl and mix. Stir in the orange rind, sultanas and nuts. Add the orange juice, buttermilk, eggs, molasses and oil and stir well. Pour mixture into muffin tins, filling them 2/3 full and bake for 25 minutes.

Cookies with chocolate chips

75 grams soft butter
100 grams caster sugar

70 grams light brown sugar

1 large egg, room temperature

2 tsp of orange extract

Plain white flour or white spelt flour

1 tsp of bicarbonate of soda

175 grams dark chocolate chips

Or

50 grams (in total) of hazelnuts and/or walnuts

125 grams dark chocolate chips

Preheat oven to 160°C/180°F/Gas 3.

Beat together the soft butter and both sugars until pale and fluffy.

Add the egg and orange extract, beat to combine.

In another bowl, sift the flour and bicarbonate of soda. Gradually add the creamed mixture into the bowl beating lightly, fold in the chocolate chips/nuts, whatever you fancy, but make sure it's the right amount.

Bake for 10-12 minutes. Take out of oven and leave on the tray for about 10 minutes.

Transfer onto a wire rack. Cookies will feel soft but will firm when cooled.

Mumma's minestrone soup

3 chopped onions

4 crushed garlic cloves

1 finely chopped celeriac root

3 tbsp olive oil

500g chopped tomatoes

1 green and 1 yellow pepper, finely chopped and de-seeded

4 pints chicken stock

6 to 8 carrots diced

1 cup tomato paste

1 tsp fresh oregano

1 tsp fresh basil

1 tsp fresh rosemary

Salt and pepper to taste

Take a large saucepan and gently fry the onions, garlic and celeriac in olive oil. Next add the tomatoes and simmer for five minutes. Then add the rest of the vegetables and herbs. Lastly add the tomato paste.

Simmer for two hours.

Personally, ten minutes before serving, I like to add one cup of pasta stars and a handful of parsley.

Serves at least six.

Grandma's recipe for Moules Mariniere

Mussels (enough for 4 servings, ask fishmonger)
1 cup of butter
4 cloves of garlic
1 litre white wine
1 handful chopped parsley

Clean the mussels in a lot of water to get rid of any grit (make sure you throw away any that are not fully closed). In a saucepan, melt the butter, add finely chopped garlic and parsley, then pour in the white wine and lastly, add the mussels.

Cook in the saucepan for about 15 minutes or until open and serve with plenty of bread and butter.

Serves four.

Sole

1 fresh clean sole (1 sole per person)
½ cup butter
2 tbsp flour
1 lemon
2 tbsp fresh chopped parsley
Salt and pepper to taste

On a plate mix the flour with salt and pepper. Melt the butter in a frying pan. Place the fish onto the plate with the flour on it and cover both sides. Put the fish into the pan and fry until golden on both sides. Cut the lemon in half and squeeze over the cooked fish.

Serve with chopped parsley and mashed potatoes.

Wild garlic pesto

1 small bunch of wild garlic leaves (about 20 leaves)

8 sprigs of basil, or if you prefer, watercress, spinach or rocket – whatever you fancy.

15 large walnuts

40 grams of sheep cheese or parmesan cheese

Several very generous glugs of olive oil.

Combine all ingredients in a blender.

It will keep in the fridge for two weeks, just make sure you put it into a glass jar with a lid. Cover the top of the pesto with olive oil, that will keep it fresh. You can also freeze it – put the pesto into small containers if you need smaller portions.

Onion soup

25 grams butter

2 tbsp olive oil

5 finely sliced large onions

1.5 litre chicken stock

1 cup grated gruyere cheese

1 cup croutons (toasted French bread)

Pepper to taste

Heat the butter and olive oil in a saucepan. Add onions and cook slowly over low heat until translucent, but do not brown. Add the chicken stock and season.
Simmer for 20 minutes.
Top with French bread slices covered in gruyere cheese and leave to melt. Is also delicious with aioli sauce (see page x).
Serves two.

Peter's hash browns

700 grams potatoes peeled and grated

2 cloves of crushed garlic

Dash of Worcestershire sauce

A little olive oil
Salt and pepper to taste

Heat the olive oil in a frying pan and add the grated potatoes, garlic and seasoning. Cook over a medium heat until brown underneath. When ready, turn (I put a lid on top and turn over) and cook until crisp and golden.

Serve on a heated plate with anything you like. It goes very well with a full English breakfast!

Serves about four.

Porridge

400 ml water
200 ml oat flakes

Put ingredients into a saucepan and boil gently, stirring all the time.
Serve with double cream, apples and honey.
Serves about two.

Rikke's chocolate cake

225 grams butter
225 grams chocolate (72% cocoa solids) broken into pieces
150 grams sugar
100 grams flour
1 large teaspoon of instant coffee
3 separated eggs
100 grams freshly chopped almonds or walnuts

Put the almonds into a bowl and cover with boiling water. Leave for 30 minutes and remove the skin. If using walnuts this isn't necessary.

Put the butter and chocolate into a heatproof bowl. Heat water in a saucepan and add the heatproof bowl, melt the butter and chocolate over a low heat (this is called a Bain Marie). Remove the saucepan from the heat and leave to cool. Then pour in the sugar, flour, coffee, three egg yolks and chopped nuts.

In another bowl, whisk three egg whites until very stiff, then add to the mixture in the saucepan and stir very gently.

Butter the cake-tin and pour the mixture in.

Bake in the oven at 150°C/300°F/Gas 3 for 50-55 minutes.

Serve with whipped cream or creme fraiche.

Vegetarian Lasagne

16 strips of lasagne

3 lbs frozen spinach

½ lb butter

2 tsp oregano (fresh if possible)

1.5 lbs Ricotta cheese

1 lb chopped leeks

lb chopped onions Olive oil

Salt and pepper to taste.

For the sauce

8oz sliced mushrooms

1.5 pints vegetable stock

½ lb grated Leicester or pecorino cheese

3 packets sliced mozzarella cheese

First of all, thaw the spinach. Into a large saucepan pour a little olive oil. When warm, add the onions and leeks. Cook until transparent. Add the spinach and oregano. When cool, stir in the ricotta cheese.

Cook the lasagne strips and put aside.

Melt the butter in another saucepan and add the mushrooms. Cook covered for five minutes. Add the stock and season to taste. Cook for another five minutes.

Pour some oil into the oven dish and layer the spinach mixture with the lasagne strips. Repeat layers and finish with the mushrooms on the top. Cover with mozzarella cheese and lastly sprinkle Leicester or pecorino cheese on top.

Bake in the oven on the middle shelf on 150°C/300°F/Gas 3 for 35-40 minutes until golden.

Serve with a crisp green salad.

Serves eight.

Spare ribs

Ask your local butcher to cut the rack of ribs into separate ribs. Marinate the ribs overnight in this sauce.

Sauce

In a bowl mix together the following ingredients:

Juice of 1 lemon and 1 lime
1 cup of honey

3 tbsp sweet chilli sauce
4 tbsp brown sugar
½ cup balsamic vinegar
1 cup tomato paste
½ cup Kikkoman sauce
4 cloves crushed garlic
1 cup water
2 tsp of mustard
Salt and pepper to taste
Preheat the oven to 220°C/Gas mark 7.

Put the ribs in the oven for 15 minutes at 250°C/450°F/Gas 7 and then lower the heat to 150°C/300°F/Gas 2 – Cover the ribs with foil and cook for a further two hours.

15 minutes before you are ready to serve the ribs take the foil cover off and let brown.

Serve with mashed potatoes and salad.

Serves about four.

Shepherd's pie
Filling

1 lb minced lamb
½ chopped celery root (optional)
2 finely chopped onions
2 large grated carrots

1 chopped green or yellow pepper
1 chopped apple (optional)
½ cup tomato paste
Salt and pepper to taste

Mashed potato

3 lbs potatoes
½ cup double cream
A knob of butter
Salt and pepper to taste

Boil the potatoes until soft, drain the water, mash them (using a fork or masher) together with the cream, butter and season to taste.

Filling

Fry the chopped onions in olive oil for 10 minutes or until transparent in a saucepan. Add the minced meat, carrots, peppers, garlic, tomato paste and salt and pepper (and the apple and celery root if using). Cook for 20 minutes on the hob.

Pour the filling into an oven dish and cover with mashed potatoes. Cook for about an hour in the oven on the middle shelf – 200°C/400°F/Gas 4.

Serves four.

Tania's favourite potato salad

3lb boiled new potatoes (let them cool down)
1 cup Greek yoghurt or creme fraiche
½ cup French dressing or homemade mayonnaise
½ cup fresh chopped parsley
½ cup fresh chopped dill
½ cup fresh chopped chives
Salt and pepper to taste

Mix the ingredients for the dressing and pour over potatoes.
Serves about four.

Potato, celeriac and parsnip puree

1lb parsnip
1lb celeriac root
1lb potatoes
1 very finely chopped onion
2 tbsp brown sugar
½ cup butter
1 cup cream
Nutmeg
Salt and pepper to taste

Peel and chop the parsnips, celeriac root and potatoes and cook in boiling water for about 25 minutes, or until soft. Once cooked, drain the water, mash them all together. Add the butter, cream, onion, sugar and nutmeg and season to taste.

This puree can keep in the fridge for up to 5 days and is delicious with a fried egg on top.

Tania's zabaglione

6 egg yolks
1 cup sugar
1 glass marsala wine

Mix the egg yolks and sugar very well. Pour into a double saucepan (Bain Marie) and whisk over hot but not boiling water until it coats the back of the spoon. Stir in the marsala wine and serve immediately.

Serve with Italian macaroons.

Tacos with chilli con carne

You can buy the tortilla shells in most supermarkets.

Warm the shells in a low oven for about 20 minutes – 100°C/200°F/Gas 2 – on a baking tray.

Make chilli con carne, either with minced beef or, if vegetarian, with kidney beans.

Chilli con carne

   2 lbs minced chicken or minced beef
   ¼ cup of olive oil
   A knob of butter
   ½ cup grated cheddar cheese
   chopped lettuce
   chopped tomatoes
   chopped avocados
   chopped spring onion
   sweet chilli sauce
   sour cream

Take the minced chicken or beef and cook it in a saucepan with melted butter and olive oil. You can add some chopped onion or fresh chives. Cook this altogether for 20 to 25 minutes. This is the meat filling for the taco but if you are vegetarian, you can replace the meat with fresh avocados.

Chop the lettuce, tomatoes, avocados and spring onion into small pieces and place into separate salad bowls.

Bring the warm taco shells to the table. Fill first with some of the meat or fresh avocado if vegetarian and then some of the cheese (so it melts).

Serve two to each person and invite them to add their own extras from the separate salad bowls.

Cover with sour cream and sweet chilli sauce.

Marguerita's Mexican Chicken

   4 pieces of chicken

For the marinade:

   1 cup Kikkoman sauce
   2 lemons/limes cut into slices
   2 cups honey
   6 crushed cloves of garlic Olive oil

Salt and pepper to taste

Put the chicken pieces into an oiled oven dish and cover with the ingredients for the marinade.

Leave covered overnight in the fridge.

Put into the oven at 170°C/300°F/Gas 3 and cook for one hour.

Serve with mashed potatoes or rice.

Beef stroganoff

1 kg chopped chuck steak
200 grams button mushrooms
2 finely chopped onions
Butter or olive oil
1 cup concentrated tomato puree
4 cups sour cream
1 small glass brandy Nutmeg
Salt and pepper to taste

Heat the butter or olive oil in a saucepan and add the onions. Cook until transparent. Add the tomato puree and chopped meat. Simmer for 5 minutes.

Add mushrooms and brandy, then the nutmeg and season to taste. Cook covered very slowly for 1.5 hours – 180°C/150°F/Gas 3.

Serve with mashed potatoes and a green salad.

Serves about 4-6.

Shoulder of lamb with vegetables

1 cubed onions
2 cubed celery root
3 cubed potatoes
4 cubed carrots
4 cubed courgettes
2 cubed parsnips
1 cup chopped broad beans
1 cup of green, yellow or red pepper
Fresh oregano
3 cloves of crushed garlic Olive oil

Salt and pepper to taste

Put some olive oil into a casserole dish along with all the vegetables. Place the lamb on top. Cover and put on the middle shelf of the oven at 150°C/300°F/Gas 3 for three hours.

Serve with mustard and mint sauce.

Serves six.

Tania's French dressing coleslaw

For the dressing:

2 tbsp white wine vinegar

2 tbsp olive oil

4 tbsp sunflower oil

1.5 tsp Dijon mustard

1.5 tsp white sugar

1 crushed clove of garlic (optional)

Juice of ½ a lemon

Mix the mustard, vinegar, sugar, lemon and garlic (if using). Slowly add the oil, this will help emulsify the dressing.

For the coleslaw:

1 small red or white cabbage

1 small onion

4 carrots

1 apple

mayonnaise

1 tsp caraway seeds

Shred the cabbage, grate the carrots and finely chop the onion and apple. Combine the ingredients with the French dressing in a mixing bowl, mix well, cover and chill until required.

Beetroot, garlic and parsley salad

1.5 lbs of beetroot, (you can buy ready cooked beetroot.) if you prefer.

6 stems of celery

1 apple

2/3 cloves of garlic

Handful of parsley finely chopped

Clean and trim the beetroot. Cook them for 30 mins. Peel the skin off while still warm. Cut the beetroot, apple and celery into small cubes.

Make a French Dressing.

3 tbs of extra virgin olive oil, you can also use rapeseed oil

Finely grated Zest of ½ lemon

2 tbs of lemon juice

½ tsp of English mustard

1 tsp of runny honey

Salt and pepper to taste

Mix together in a bowl and gently toss the garlic on top. Pour the dressing in a jug so friends can help themselves.

Watercress and avocado salad

1 large bunch of fresh watercress, washed and torn

2 large chopped ripe avocados

3 grated carrots

Handful of sultanas

Handful of roasted sesame seeds

Juice of 1 lemon

Take sesame seeds and put them in a dry frying pan over a low heat on the hob. As soon as you can smell they are cooking or look golden, take them off.

Combine all of the ingredients and sprinkle the lemon juice over the salad.

Place in the fridge until ready to serve.

The lemon juice also stops the avocados from discolouring.

Polenta

I use pre-cooked polenta; you only need to cook it for 8 min. After cooking it you can serve it as it is, or pour it onto a flat surface, a large plate or baking tray.

Once ready, leave to cool and then cut into slices and brush with a little olive oil. Season with salt and pepper. If you want to sprinkle on some herbs, do.

Put under the hot grill and turn over when crisp and light brown. When both sides are done serve with tomato sauce (see recipe on page x).

Homemade tomato sauce

3 tbsp olive oil
3 medium red onions, peeled and sliced very thinly and then chopped
3 cloves of grated garlic
3 lbs of plum tomatoes (fresh or tins)
Pepper and salt to taste

Heat the olive oil in a large saucepan and add the onions. Cook until see through and soft (low heat for about 35 min). Add garlic and tomatoes and cook for about two hours. Add pepper and salt to taste.

Steak in green peppercorns

1 steak per person
3-4 tsp crushed green peppercorns
250 grams double cream
100 grams butter
½ cup of brandy
1tbs cornflour
2tbs tomato puree
Salt to taste

Melt the butter in a frying pan on a low heat. Coat the steaks in the flour and cook on each side for a minute (this keeps the juice inside the steak). Mix the tomato puree and cornflour with the cream and brandy. Take the frying pan off the heat and cover the steaks with the cream mixture. Let this stand for 2-3 hours.

Before reheating in the frying pan, pour on the crushed peppercorns. Cook for another five minutes in this way.

Delicious served with chips and a crunchy green salad.

Remoulade

1 large cup of Greek yoghurt
2 shallots
2 cox apples
4 pickled dill cucumbers
1.5 tbsp mango chutney
½ tsp of curry powder
½ tsp sugar
Salt and pepper to taste

Pour all ingredients into a blender and blend until smooth and then refrigerate.

This is a very useful sauce and can be served with anything from a meat fondue to a cheese sandwich.

French toast

4 slices of bread (crusts removed)
2 eggs (lightly beaten)
4 tbsp single cream
50 grams butter

Mix the eggs and cream together and dip the bread into the mixture. Melt the butter in the frying pan. Take the soaked slices of bread and fry for 1-2 minutes on each side.

If you want a sweet dish then add some nutmeg and maple syrup. Otherwise, if you want a savoury dish, then season with salt and pepper and serve with bacon.

Mushroom and garlic pate

50 grams of olive oil
225 grams finely chopped mushrooms

2 finely chopped leeks

1 finely chopped onion

1 small tin of chickpeas (rinsed and drained)

3 crushed cloves of garlic

A handful of chopped parsley

A pinch of oregano

Pepper to taste

Pour olive oil into a saucepan and cook the onion and leeks until transparent. Next add the mushrooms garlic and parsley (stirring all the time). Season. Liquidise the chick peas and pour them into the saucepan with the mushrooms. Stir well and put them into a dish and then cover with clarified butter (butter that has been melted in a saucepan).

Chill in the fridge overnight.

French Peasant Dish

1 lb leeks prepared and chopped

2 cups mushrooms washed and sliced

2 cups Leicester cheese

2 cups single cream Juice of ½ a lemon handful of parsley

1 cup of stock or water

A little olive oil or butter

½ cup wine

Salt and pepper to taste

5 slices of bread (crusts removed)

Put the oil or butter into a saucepan and add the vegetables. Simmer for five minutes. Pour in the stock, cream, lemon and wine and add then and the parsley. Season to taste.

Line a baking dish with three slices of bread and pour the vegetables in. Put the other two slices of bread on top and cover with the cheese.

Cook for about 30 minutes in a medium oven – 200°C/400°F/Gas 4.

This is really scrumptious on a cold winter's night in front of the fire with a glass of red wine!

David's toffee potatoes

2 lbs small new potatoes washed, peeled, boiled and cooled

2 cups of sugar

2 cups of butter

2 tbsp water

Put the sugar into a frying pan and cook until golden but not too dark. Add the butter and stir together very gently.

Put the boiled, cooled potatoes in a colander and put under a cold tap briefly. Shake off any excess water. Add to the toffee mixture. Using a wooden spoon coat the potatoes well with the toffee.

When the potatoes have become brown on all sides add 2tbs of water and mix well. Make sure to keep the potatoes warm until ready to serve.

My Pancakes

2 large eggs

¾ cup unbleached white flour

1⅓ cup milk

3 tbsp butter

Pinch of salt (optional)

Combine the eggs, milk and flour in a blender. Put some butter into a frying pan and pour in a small amount of batter. Cook over a medium heat until golden and turn.

These are a real treat when served with fresh blueberries or sliced white peaches.

Fish Pie

1.5 lb fresh, cooked and chopped haddock or cod fillets

1 large handful of clean, cooked, peeled prawns or scampi

3 lb mashed potatoes

2 finely chopped onions

1 egg (optional)

2 cups cream

½ cup white wine

2 tbsp fresh dill

A handful of fresh parsley

Juice of 1 lemon

A little butter or oil

Salt and pepper to taste

Place the fish and prawns/scampi into a buttered baking dish. Mix together finely chopped onions, wine, dill, parsley, lemon, salt and pepper. Add this to the dish. Cover with foil and put into the oven for 20 minutes at 180°C/350°F/Gas 4.

Next mix the mashed potatoes with the cream.

Take the dish out of the oven and add ⅔ of the potatoes to the fish. The rest you put on top.

Whisk the egg, pour over potatoes and place in the oven for a further 20 minutes at the same temperature.

Serve with a salad.

Serves about four.

Very easy spelt bread

Preheat oven to 220°C/430°F/Gas 5.

300 gram spelt flour

200 gram all-purpose flour

380 ml of lukewarm water

1 tsp of dried yeast

2 tsp of honey

1.5 tsp of salt

A handful of oats for dusting on top (if you would like)

Mix the two flours into a bowl. Add yeast, water and honey until mixed. Next add the salt and mix well using a spoon. Mix until all ingredients have come together. If dough is dry, add a tiny bit of water.

Rise one:

Leave the dough covered with a damp tea towel for about two hours, or until it has doubled in size.

Rise two:

Dust your work surface with flour, put the risen dough on it (using floured hands as dough very sticky). Next place it onto a baking tray and leave for 1.5 hours, covered with a tea towel.

After dough has risen for the 2nd time, dust with oats.

Fill a heatproof bowl of hot water and put this in the oven to create some steam as this helps the dough to get a good crust.

Put the dough into the oven on the baking tray for eight to ten minutes, then turn the oven down to around 200°C/390°F/Gas 4.

Bake for 35 to 40 minutes, until golden brown. Cool on wire rack.

Leave a while before slicing

Tomato and pine nut accompaniment (this is lovely to put on top of fish)

4 large tomatoes cut into small pieces

1 cup of raisins (that you have left overnight in white wine or sherry)

1 cup of pine nuts that you have roasted lightly

1 cup of parsley

½ cup of olive oil

Salt and pepper to taste.

Mix all the ingredients together with ½ a cup of olive oil and serve.

Macaroni cheese

Preheat oven to Gas 6/200°C/400°F/Gas 6.

1 litre of full cream milk

350 grams of macaroni or penne pasta (or any short-dried pasta)

60 grams butter

60 grams plain flour

200 grams grated pecorino or Manchego cheese (keep 4 tbsp of cheese to toss over with the breadcrumbs)

80 grams breadcrumbs

Mustard to taste

Pinch of salt (as cheese quite salty) and pepper

Cook pasta until tender, about seven to eight minutes, and drain using a colander.

Melt the butter in a saucepan, add flour slowly to make a paste. Gradually pour in the milk and whisk till all the lumps have gone. Pour in the grated cheese. Add the grained mustard. Fold in the drained pasta.

Tip all into a large heatproof dish (or gratin dish).

Toss the grated cheese and breadcrumbs on top.

Bake for about 35 to 40 minutes – until golden on top.

Serves four people.

Auntie Mette's Thai fish soup

2 cloves of garlic, grated

2 onions, cut into very small pieces

2 green or red chilli (depends on how strong you like it) cut into tiny pieces

Small piece of ginger (about ½ a finger)

Lemongrass to taste

1-2 tsp of red curry paste

1.5 litres of chicken broth (buy this in the shop)

Put everything into the saucepan with 1.5 litres of chicken broth.

And a whole tin of coconut milk. Season with a squeeze of lemon or lime. Cook on a medium heat.

You can put in chicken pieces, or pieces of fish. Whatever you fancy.

Serves two.

Beetroot Soup

60 grams butter

2 onions chopped

1 large carrot chopped

2 sticks celery chopped

1 apple peeled and chopped

4 cloves of garlic chopped very fine

800 grams beetroot trimmed, peeled and sliced (you can cook them yourself or buy them cooked)

2 litres of chicken or vegetable stock

Chopped parsley or chopped watercress

Melt the butter in the saucepan. Add the onions, carrots, celery, apple and garlic. 'Sweat' for 20 minutes until onion is soft and see through. Add the sliced beetroot.

Cover again and sweat for another 20 minutes. Bring to the boil and simmer until everything is tender. Leave to cool then puree in the mixer or with a hand whisk.

Add seasoning to taste along with the chopped parsley and olive oil, you can also use chopped watercress.

Serve in a bowl with crumbled goat cheese or any cheese you like.

Serves about 2-3 people.

Green Juice

1 cup of water
½ juice of lemon or lime
1 pear
2 sticks of celery
Ginger (a finger)
1 avocado
½ cup of broccoli

Place together in blender, drink and enjoy!

How To Have A Good Dinner Party

Chapter 7:
How to Have a Good
Dinner Party

My mother was always entertaining friends and I have very fond memories of a cosy home with delicious food and lovely people.

Going out to restaurants is always a treat, of course, but there's something special about inviting friends you care about into your home and enjoying a nice home-cooked meal together.

It just takes a little time, effort…and love.

I have included everything you need to know about how to entertain. Even if you are just having a few friends around for a bowl of spaghetti, the important thing is not to panic and just use what is relevant for that evening…and plan.

It's good to be organised. The first thing you need to do is work out when you want to have people over for supper and then who you want to invite.

Decide on what your guests would like to eat and make sure you are aware of any dietary requirements or food intolerances/allergies.

Make sure you have enough plates, bowls and cutlery to go around.

Once you have decided what you are going to cook, make sure you have everything you need for the recipe and decide whether you can make it on the day or if more preparation is needed.

Make sure that there is enough oven space for the food you've decided to cook, so there won't be any nasty last-minute surprises.

Make sure that you have enough ice.

If you have food that was prepared the day before, make sure to take it out of the fridge/freezer.

Put all drinks that need to be chilled into the fridge.

Make the rest of the food, cover with foil or clingfilm and keep cool.

Lay the table and make sure you have enough chairs for everyone.

Check bathroom and hang a clean towel.

Make the salad, cover and keep cool (if serving).

Pour salad dressing into a jug.

Make sure that you have enough soft drinks.

Make sure that you have sparkling and still water.

Take the corks out of the red and white wine (if you are serving it) and let it 'breathe'.

Have a bath/shower and get dressed into something that makes you feel happy.

Of course you may not have all that time to prepare, or the party may be a spontaneous idea. If so, keep it simple and try to pack the preparation tips I've suggested into whatever time you have.

Good luck!

Whether you're the host or a guest I have two final pieces of advice…

As a host, plan well, make sure every guest feels special and don't panic.

As a guest, arrive on time and in a good mood, sing for your supper, don't outstay your welcome and please don't ask, "Did you make this yourself?"

Most of all have fun!

Towards a
Healthy you

AND
A BEAUTIFUL AND
HANDSOME YOU.

Chapter 8: Towards a Healthy You and a Beautiful and Handsome You

A Healthy You

If you feel good you look good.

To help you achieve this, here are some thoughts:

1. Keep hydrated – when you get up in the morning drink a glass of water with a slice of lemon. And keep drinking water – up to two litres a day is fine. I believe you can't ever drink too much water but try not to drink water from a plastic bottle because the plastic is very bad for you. Invest in a glass bottle that you refill and keep in the fridge or a good quality metal water bottle flask.
2. Try not to eat too much salt and sugar.
3. Eat a healthy breakfast – It's the most important meal of the day which will kick-start your metabolism and sets you up for the day. Why not try any of these: scrambled or boiled eggs, avocado, toast, muesli and yoghurt, porridge, fresh fruit, a cup of tea or coffee, a glass of fresh fruit juice, oatcakes with cheese and avocado is delicious.
4. Don't skip meals – Try eating breakfast like a king, lunch like a prince and supper like a pauper. Could be something of a challenge when you return home ravenous at the end of the day, but just give it a go when you can.
5. Try not to drink too much alcohol – a glass of red or white wine a day is acceptable. However, do not drink and drive.
6. Don't smoke or vape!

7. Try to find an exercise regime that suits you. They say just 20 minutes of dedicated exercise three times a week is good for you. I like to do it at home, but if you prefer, find a gym where you feel comfortable that's just as wonderful. However, there's really no need to join a gym when there are plenty of fitness programmes online and fitness programme apps, anyway, walking is one of the best exercises around. Why not find yourself an exercise buddy – great for upping the commitment factor and you'll be able to motivate one another.

8. Try yoga – there are many different styles around, from Slow Flow and Restorative to a more 'dynamic' practice and it's great for body, mind and soul.

9. Sleep well – try to have eight hours of sleep; some people need more, some less. However, as a general rule, your body needs eight hours to regenerate.

Remember, these are just suggestions. We're all individuals and you'll soon find out what works best for your own health.

Find yourself a doctor, dentist and optician – you'll need to know where you can go to have your eyes tested regularly. It's important to register with these people so you know where to go either for check-ups or when you need urgent help.

It's all too easy to neglect or forget to make these appointments when it's all down to you. Boring, maybe – essential, definitely.

Finally, so much has been written about vitamins and mineral supplements with views ranging from how they can help to how they can be a complete waste of time. The fact is you should be able to get most of the vitamins and minerals you need if you make sure you eat a balanced diet. But that's a tall order when life is hectic.

So, I suggest you find a chemist or health store where you feel comfortable to ask advice. They'll be delighted to help and can take into consideration your age, build and life-style to be sure to suggest the right supplements for you.

Let's face it everyone's different.

A Beautiful or Handsome You

It's easy to be bamboozled and baffled by all the skincare advice that flies around, not to mention the seemingly endless stream of new skin care products for everyone that hit the shelves.

My hope is to steer you through the minefield so you can establish a skin-care regime of your own that suits you.

Face Care: Let's face it, everyone wants clear healthy-looking skin every day, and with a little care and attention, believe me, it *is* possible. So much of how your skin looks is down to what you eat, how much water you drink and your lifestyle. However, a good daily skincare regime can make all the difference, helping to ensure your skin looks and stays at its very best.

In fact, there's no great secret to having great looking skin. You just need to follow a few simple steps, whatever your skin type, whether it be normal, greasy, combination or dry.

It's pretty easy to tell what skin type you are by how it looks and feels. Greasy skin tends to shine, dry skin feels tight and can have flaky patches, and combination skin is when it's greasy across the forehead and around the nose area (often called the T-zone for obvious reasons).

However, if you're not sure what type of skin you have, go and have a chat with a skin care consultant in your local high street chemist or any department store. Ask questions and they'll be delighted to give you advice and analyse your skin properly.

Just as my mother did with me, I started looking after my children's skin from a very early age. In fact, Tania had her own skincare routine that she could do alone from the age of 11. However, my son, Peter, did not really worry about it until he was much older!

So here goes.

Four steps to great looking skin:

1. Clean thoroughly
2. Moisturise
3. Exfoliate regularly
4. Be vigilant about how much time you spend in the sun

Step 1: Cleanse, cleanse, cleanse...

Cleanse morning and night, although it's more important to thoroughly cleanse before bed to remove all traces of the day's dirt or make-up, a quick wash or splash of cold water first thing freshens up your skin.

Whether you use a wash that rinses off or a lotion with cotton pads or a cloth, please make sure your skin is squeaky clean – your towel will tell you soon enough whether you've done a good job or not!

If you wear mascara, especially waterproof, it's wise to use an eye make-up remover. It's tempting to rub away but that's bad news for the delicate skin around the eye area. Instead drench a cotton wool pad in the eye make-up remover, press onto the lashes with your eyes closed, leave for a second or two and then gently wipe away. You may need to repeat this action depending on how effective your remover is.

It's not essential to use a toner – which is just lotion often with a mild astringent – but it can help remove the last traces of dirt and make-up. And if you have oily skin, a toner can help control excess greasiness and shine.

Wipes have become big news and are hugely popular. No surprise, the idea of a quick wipe-and-go is extremely appealing. However, they don't do a thorough job so only use in an emergency and are not at all environmentally friendly.

Step 2: Moisturise

Most skin needs moisturiser to keep it soft and supple – even oily skin. Keeping skin cells full and plump using moisturiser also creates a barrier which helps keep out dirt and bacteria.

Choose a moisturiser to suit your skin type. There are plenty of light mousses and gels if you have oily skin – though avoid those that promise 'shine control' as the way they tend to work is by covering and blocking pores rather than treating the cause. If you have 'normal skin' or tend towards drier skin then choose a natural and creamy product.

Whilst there's no need for you to buy sophisticated and expensive anti-ageing creams, you must always use a moisturiser with a minimum SPF15 – even in winter.

Lines and wrinkles may not concern you right now, but be aware that moisturising your skin at your age will help keep your skin young-looking for many years to come. Much better to start preventing now, rather than be faced with the harder task of treatment and repair later.

Whilst we're on this subject, if you don't want a 'turkey neck' in years to come, start prevention tactics now by not stopping at your jawline with your moisturiser. Smooth in cream from the nape of your neck up to your jawline with a sweeping upwards action.

Don't forget your neck either. You'll thank me for it!

Step 3: Exfoliate Regularly

Exfoliation is simply the removal of dead cells on the skin's surface. Even though your skin sheds cells naturally, dead cells can collect leaving your complexion looking dull and lifeless. So, a little extra help is needed, say once a week, to keep skin looking bright and fresh.

There are many, many scrubs on the shelves but a flannel or muslin cloth wrung out in hot water does a very effective job. Don't be too rough, just gently rub, rinse and pat dry with a towel. Not only will your skin feel brand new but your moisturiser will work even better without a layer of dead cells to battle its way through.

It's also a good idea to also exfoliate your lips from time to time to keep them smooth, always applying a little Vaseline.

Step 4: Be vigilant about how much time you spend in the sun

Let's face it we all love the feeling of the sun and we all need a little. However, those rays are dangerous. Not only can over-exposure to the sun's rays cause skin cancer but sun-worshipping is the worst cause of ageing – along with smoking.

There are two types of ultraviolet rays – UVA rays are the ageing ones and UVB rays are the ones that burn. When you go out in the sun, choose a sunscreen that protects against both types of ultraviolet rays, apply regularly and remember UVA's can even travel through glass.

If you like a sun-tanned look sunbathe very carefully, especially if you're fair-skinned and with so many fabulous self-tanning options on the market, why not fake it. Just take care.

Whether you go for a gradual tanning cream that builds over time or a normal self-tan product the two golden rules apply for a streak-free result – exfoliate and moisturise before you apply.

However, tempting a tanning booth may seem never succumb, as they have been proven time and time again to be harmful and even dangerous.

Face Care Treats

My grandma's words still ring in my ear: "This is the only skin you'll ever have – so look after it."

With this in mind it's worth going the extra mile.

So, on top of your daily skincare routine, why not indulge your skin in regular treats? Not only will your skin benefit but it can be wonderfully relaxing after a tough week – and fun!

Buy a deep cleansing or moisturising mask, lie back with your favourite magazine and see your skin glow afterwards.

Take a little longer to apply your moisturiser, massaging your face and neck. The massaging movement stimulates circulation giving you extra radiance, it relieves tension and ensures that the moisturiser is fully absorbed. Here are a few massage techniques you could try out:

Place your fingertips in the middle of your forehead and make light sweeping movements upwards and outwards. Repeat this action from your lower cheek and moving up over your cheekbones.

Using your forefinger and middle fingers tap along your brow line from the inner eye corner outwards. Repeat along the lower eye socket and also along the jawline.

Find the apple of your cheeks and using your index finger first press and hold for a few seconds and then gently make small circular movements. With your jaw tilted upwards, and using both hands make smoothing movements the length of your neck.

Why not give yourself a mini-facial and turn your bathroom into a spa? True indulgence. Turn off your mobile, light a candle or two, put on some music, scrape back your hair and off you go. Your mini-facial will take a little time, but why not enjoy? Here goes:

1. Thoroughly cleanse, taking care to remove all dirt and make-up. Pat dry.

2. Exfoliate – go gently!

3. Steam – hold your face cloth under the hot water tap, wring it out before placing gently over your face for a few minutes, letting the steam into your pores.

4. Close pores – using a cloth rinsed with very cold water (as above).

5. Apply your mask – and lie back while it works away. Usually, masks take ten minutes but follow the instructions on the pack.

6. Rinse – taking particular care along the hair-line where masks can stick.

7. Apply moisturiser – using the massaging techniques suggested.

Puffy eyes? Just place a couple of cotton pads in a small bowl of water and pop it into your freezer for thirty minutes or so. Then put the pads on closed lids, lie back and fifteen minutes later, hey presto, wide-awake sparkling eyes again. You can also use slices of cucumber.

It's not all plain sailing as there are some specific problems that need specific attention.

Spots!

I've had spots. Everyone gets spots. And whether you have one or a few, it's all the same.

Spots have a nasty habit of pitching up just before that special party or date. Interestingly, greasy food and sweets are not the culprits. Instead, you can thank stress and your hormones for breakouts.

So let's talk prevention, treatment and when you absolutely have to camouflage.

Prevention is all about keeping pores ultra-clean. In addition to your daily routine, try steaming your face once a week for a deep-down cleanse (as recommended above).

Also, try anti-bacterial deep cleanse masks that go deep into pores to help keep skin clear from spots.

If despite all your efforts a spot appears, don't panic, and whatever you do, don't pick or squeeze. Squeezing, while it may be tempting, not only makes the spot look worse but it will take longer to heal and can spread bacteria leading to further breakouts.

Natural treatments include a dab of tea-tree oil – or rub garlic on the spot (garlic is a natural antibacterial).

No one should have to suffer persistent spots – or acne, as doctors call it – and so all GPs will be able to help you if it's a constant problem.

There are lots of over-the-counter products, so do ask your chemist for advice.

It's best to leave spots uncovered. However, the reality is that sometimes you just have to conceal a spot. Make-up can clog and make matters worse and so use an antibacterial concealer and then lightly pat with a little powder – the mineral type is best – to stop any shine.

Ultra-Dry Skin

Dry itchy skin can be as much of a problem as spots. If you suffer from eczema or very dry skin, then you need to learn how to manage it day-to-day. Avoid contact with fragranced products which will immediately irritate your skin and keep it well moisturised to help prevent itchiness and inflammation. It is worth trying out a few products that have been specifically made for eczema prone or very dry skin. You can also make an appointment with your GP if you need further help.

Hair Care

We all know what a 'bad hair' day feels like, nothing looks right or goes according to plan.

Well, I can't promise to banish bad hair days from your life but I can offer some guidance to having great-looking hair most of the time.

Just as with your skin, the health of your hair – how much it shines, how fast it grows, how strong it is, is down to genes, eating a good balanced diet and not being too stressed. However, the way you look after your hair day-to-day can make a real difference.

There are just two steps to good hair care:

Step One – Shampoo

First thing is using the right shampoo – and with so many on the shelves this is no mean feat. The reality is you may need to try a few to find the one that suits you best.

So, what kind of hair do you have? Unsure? Well, a quick guide is that if your hair looks like it needs washing every morning then it's greasy, if it's flyaway and prone to splitting then it's dry. If you have a greasy scalp and dry ends then go for a gentle shampoo. And if your hair looks and behaves well for a few days then you're lucky, your hair is normal.

Please don't choose a shampoo because it is ultra-cheap. Some of the bargain basket lines are nothing more than detergent, which, whatever your hair type, can cause damage by stripping out natural oils. Think of them as using washing up liquid on your crowning glory – you wouldn't want that would you?

Give yourself a really good shampoo to thoroughly cleanse away dirt and grease. You only need a little shampoo. Use your fingertips to really work all around, not forgetting around your face where make-up can build in the hairline. Not only are you cleaning your hair but stimulating your scalp. Rinse until the water is clear and your hair squeaks.

Whether you wash your hair once or twice is down to you and just how dirty your hair is. Also, if you tend to use lots of styling products it can be a good idea to have a second shampoo to make sure all the gunk has been removed properly – before you start again! No need to buy a special 'detoxing' shampoo as your regular one should do as good a job.

How often you wash your hair is again completely down to you.

I'd like to dispel a few myths.

It is neither good nor bad for you to wash your hair every day. If you use a gentle shampoo washing daily doesn't harm hair, nor does it benefit it in anyway, apart from giving you that 'just-washed' feeling.

However, daily washing can get you into a 'high maintenance' habit that can frankly be a bore and also because you have become so used to just washed hair you can think that your hair 'needs' washing every day.

If you're caught in this 'wash every day' cycle, but want to break out of it, if you can bear it, leave your hair for as long as possible. You'll find that after a few days you'll get used to it and you're allowing your own natural oils to add shine and bounce to your hair.

You don't have to change shampoos because your hair suffers 'shampoo fatigue'. This really is twaddle.

Step Two – Always Use Conditioner? No, I Don't!

Mistakenly, it's often thought that conditioners make hair greasy. This simply is not the case. A conditioner smooths down your hair's follicles making it look shinier and feel softer whilst also detangling so that combing through is a whole lot easier.

As long as you rinse thoroughly leaving no residue, a conditioner, far from leaving your hair lank and lifeless, will help give you the glossiness and silky feel we all want.

If you are prone to having greasy hair, however, you may consider just smoothing conditioner onto the ends of your hair with just a dab on the scalp area.

And if you have dry hair go for an intense conditioning session when you have the time. You can buy special conditioning masks, but it's not essential. When you've finished shampooing give your hair a quick towel dry, then apply your conditioner massaging it in all over and leave for ten minutes or so. Rinse thoroughly and comb through. This treatment is also worth doing if you use lots of styling products, blow-dry consistently or use heated rollers or straighteners – all of which can dry out and damage the shaft of your hair affecting how it looks and feels.

If you don't feel like using conditioner, you can add half a cup of vinegar into a pint of warm winter and pour onto your hair – it will make your hair shine!

Body Care

So important: Wash hands making sure you clean in between your fingers and the back of your hand.

It's not enough to stop at face-care as the skin on your body needs a little love and attention too.

The face-care four steps of cleansing, moisturising, exfoliating regularly and keeping out of the sun all apply to body-care too.

In addition, there are a few extras that will ensure your body looks and feels its best.

Dry Brushing: My mother was a great fan of dry brushing and did it without fail every day. Dry brushing is a great habit to get into as not only does it boost circulation, remove dead cells and make your skin glow, but it also builds your immune system warding off germs and bacteria. You'll need a long handled stiff natural bristle brush and you do this when your skin is completely dry – so before or after a bath or shower.

Start at your feet and with gentle movements, stroking upwards. Work up to your knee, then from your knee to your thigh. Then start at your fingertips and work up to your elbows and then up to your shoulders. Don't forget your back.

Make sure you brush upwards and towards your heart rather than away.

Finish by placing the brush on your stomach and making small circular movements.

Super hydration: When you've showered or had a bath, dry naturally or just pat yourself with a towel. Apply your body oil or lotion whilst your skin is still a little damp to help seal the moisture in and to have the best results.

A beautifully clear back: Backs can be prone to spots and are notoriously tricky to reach to clean properly. Invest in a long handled soft natural bristle brush which you dampen with cleanser or soap and gently rub backwards and forwards. Be sure to rinse well.

Just as with exfoliation, you'll find that your moisturiser absorbs more effectively after a good body brushing session. Try it and I guarantee you'll be hooked!

Super smooth elbows and knees: Especially in winter, elbows and knees need extra attention to keep them from becoming dry. Exfoliate regularly and smooth-in an extra-large dollop of cream afterwards to keep skin supple and protected.

Hands and feet: Hands and feet have a hard time of it and yet so often skincare regimes treat them as the poor cousin to our faces and bodies. Take a little time to keep yours feeling loved and looking good.

Hands: Hands are a real giveaway about a person – and I'm not simply talking your age – so be sure your hands say the right things about you!

You can buy products that taste vile to help you stop biting nails, but sometimes motivation is the best trick, however, to get yourself started, paint on some translucent natural colour just to give some shine at the tips of your fingers and then, when you have the temptation to nibble, hopefully you'll be reminded of what's to come...

It may sound like a bore but try to get into the habit of applying a little hand cream daily, especially after your hands have been in water. If you have some cream left on your hands after you've moisturised your face, that will do just as well. Take extra care to work the cream into your cuticles to keep them soft rather than rough and therefore more prone to splitting.

There are special heavy-duty hand creams that offer protection, especially in cold conditions, and even repair cracked and chaffed skin. I always try to remember to keep a tube of hand cream in my bag.

If you want to give your hands a special treat, why not put a few drops of almond oil (assuming you are not allergic to almonds!) into a bowl of water and soak away. Or drench your hands in a super-rich hand cream before you go to bed, pop on some cotton gloves and you wake up with the softest hands ever.

Sometimes nails can look yellowish. A great way to freshen them up is to soak your fingertips in some fresh lemon juice which acts as a natural bleach.

I don't know anyone who doesn't love having a manicure. It's really pampering, but they can become a little expensive. It's easy enough to do your own manicure, you may be a little shaky at first but with practice will become perfect.

The DIY Manicure

Just follow these steps and enjoy the results.

1. Remove any old nail varnish.
2. Trim your nails either with scissors or clippers and then file into the shape you like.
3. Rub a little cuticle cream into the nail beds and soak in warm water for a few minutes. Pat dry, then gently push down the cuticles with your fingers, or with a cuticle stick. If your cuticles are long then you may need to carefully cut them with some nail clippers.
4. Buff the nails with a nail buffer to even the surface.
5. Massage in hand cream. Take your time to work the cream into the skin until it is fully absorbed.
6. Wipe the nails with a little soapy water to remove traces of hand cream.
7. Apply a base coat to smooth the nail surface further and also protect from colour discolouration from the nail varnish. Allow a moment to dry.

8. Apply two coats of nail polish to get the full effect of the colour and finish. The first coat is like a guide. Avoiding the cuticles, try first painting a line down the centre of the nail followed by two each side. This should cover the nail and give an elegant look without any varnish on the skin. Allow five or so minutes between coats.

9. Finish with a layer of top coat for fast drying, colour protection and extra glossiness.

Handy hint: To keep your manicure looking glossy and fresh, apply a thin layer of top coat every few days.

Feet: There aren't many people around who like their feet, but remember they do an amazing job carrying your whole body, day in and day out. Bear this in mind, so rather than become self-conscious about your feet, instead make them the best they can be and show them with confidence. After all, it would be a shame to have to limit your shoe choice!

My mother was a great believer in sea salt's natural healing and softening properties. So, I suggest you try dissolving some natural sea salt into a bowl of warm water and soak your feet for a good twenty minutes. The sea salt will soften the skin as well as soothing tired feet.

Better still before bedtime, smother your feet with a special foot cream, heavy moisturiser or oil, pop on a pair of light cotton socks. This works a treat if you need results fast.

Even just smoothing your body lotion into your feet after a bath or shower will help keep the skin soft and in good condition.

Of course, a pedicure is the best all-round treatment for feet. However, having regular professional pedicures can become pretty expensive, especially in the summer when our feet are on show more often and need to look extra good.

Pedicures are a bit trickier than manicures to do at home, but with practice you'll be able to achieve salon standard results. Here's how...

The DIY Pedicure

Follow these 13 steps to fabulous feet:

1. Remove any old varnish.
2. Soak your feet in a bowl of warm – hot water (you can add sea-salt or a drop of oil if you like).
3. Pat dry and cut the nails short with clippers or scissors and file smooth. Keep the nail line straight to avoid them becoming ingrown.
4. Apply a little cuticle oil into the nail beds and re-soak.
5. Pat dry and remove any hard skin especially on the heels and under pad using a foot scrubber or pumice stone.
6. Then gently push down the cuticles either using your fingernail or an orange stick with its end covered with a little cotton wool. Try to avoid having to cut the cuticle but if they're particularly long then carefully use cuticle trimmers to finish.
7. Pop your feet back into the water.
8. Pat dry and apply foot scrub rubbing it in, all over. Re-soak.
9. Pat dry and massage with cream taking time to work it in between the toes, around the nails and into the heel area. Enjoy the sensation of massaging your feet, over the instep and under the arch.
   Remove any traces of cream from nails with nail varnish remover.
10. Pop on a toe separator or twist tissue between each toe.
11. Apply a base-coat.
12. Apply two coats of nail colour leaving a few minutes between each application to allow nails to dry a little.
13. Paint on top coat and leave to dry for at least an hour – and avoid wearing tight shoes for even longer.

There's so much information being bombarded at us on body-care that sometimes it's hard to make sense of things. With the intelligence and common-sense you've been blessed with you will find out what works for you.

I hope these thoughts have helped.

First Aid.

Chapter 9: First Aid

(Contains public sector information licensed under the Open Government Licence v3.0.)

You may find yourself needing to deal with serious situations before medical help arrives. So here, I have outlined some of the first aid skills you should know.

I suggest that you also download the British Red Cross First Aid app onto your phone – you never know when you might need it!

Adult: https://www.redcross.org.uk/first-aid/first-aid-apps#ap p
Baby and Child: https://apps.apple.com/gb/app/baby-and-child-first-aid/id6 46471621

WHAT TO DO IF A PERSON IS UNRESPONSIVE

1. **Check breathing by tilting their head back and looking and feeling for breaths.**
   If someone is not moving and does not respond when you call them or gently shake their shoulders, they are unresponsive.
   When a person is unresponsive, their muscles relax and their tongue can block their airway so they can no longer breathe. Tilting their head back opens the airway by pulling the tongue forward.
   If they are not breathing, their chest and stomach will not be moving and you will not hear or feel their breaths.
   If they are not breathing, move on to step two.

2. **Call 999 as soon as possible.**
   If you can't call 999, get someone else to do it.

3. **Give chest compressions: push firmly downwards in the middle of the chest and then release.**

Continue to push in this way at a regular rate until help arrives.

These are called chest compressions. Chest compressions keep blood pumping around their body helping to keep the vital organs, including the brain, alive.

Keep going until help arrives.

Hands-only CPR

To carry out a chest compression:

1.	Place the heel of your hand on the breastbone at the centre of the person's chest. Place your other hand on top of your first hand and interlock your fingers.
2.	Position yourself with your shoulders above your hands.
3.	Using your body weight (not just your arms), press straight down by 5-6 cm (2 to 2.5 inches) on their chest.
4.	Keeping your hands on their chest, release the compression and allow the chest to return to its original position.
5.	Repeat these compressions at a rate of 100 to 120 times a minute until an ambulance arrives or you become exhausted.

When you call for an ambulance, telephone systems now exist that can give basic life-saving instructions, including advice about CPR.

These are now common and are easily accessible with mobile phones.

CPR with rescue breaths

If you have been trained in CPR, including rescue breaths, and feel confident using your skills, you should give chest compressions with rescue breaths.

If you're not completely confident, attempt hands-only CPR instead.

Adults

1. Place the heel of your hand on the centre of the person's chest, then place the other hand on top and press down by 5-6 cm (2 to 2.5 inches) at a steady rate of 100 to 120 compressions a minute.

2. After every 30 chest compressions, give two rescue breaths.

3. Tilt the casualty's head gently and lift the chin up with two fingers. Pinch the person's nose. Seal your mouth over their mouth, and blow steadily and firmly into their mouth for about one second. Check that their chest rises. Give two rescue breaths.

4. Continue with cycles of 30 chest compressions and two rescue breaths until they begin to recover or emergency help arrives.

Children over one year old

1.	Open the child's airway by placing one hand on their forehead and gently tilting their head back and lifting the chin. Remove any visible obstructions from the mouth and nose.
2.	Pinch their nose. Seal your mouth over their mouth, and blow steadily and firmly into their mouth, checking that their chest rises. Give five initial rescue breaths.
3.	Place the heel of one hand on the centre of their chest and push down by diameter. The quality (depth) of chest compressions is very important. Use two hands if you can't achieve a depth of 5cm using one hand.
4.	After every 30 chest compressions at a rate of 100 to 120 a minute, give two breaths.
5.	Continue with cycles of 30 chest compressions and two rescue breaths until they begin to recover or emergency help arrives.

1.	Open the infant's airway by placing one hand on their forehead and gently tilting the head back and lifting the chin. Remove any visible
2.	Place your mouth over the mouth and nose of the infant and blow steadily and firmly into their mouth, checking that their chest rises. Give five initial rescue breaths.
3.	Place two fingers in the middle of the chest and push down by 4cm (about 1.5 inches), which is approximately one-third of the chest diameter. The quality (depth) of chest compressions is very important. Use the heel of one hand if you can't achieve a depth of four cm using the tips of two fingers.
4.	After 30 chest compressions at a rate of 100 to 120 a minute, give two rescue breaths.
5.	Continue with cycles of 30 chest compressions and two rescue breaths until they begin to recover or emergency help arrives.

WHAT TO DO IF A PERSON IS RESPONSIVE

1. **Check their breathing by tilting their head back and looking and feeling for breaths.**
   If they are breathing, you will see their chest moving   and you may hear their breath or feel it on your cheek.
   If they are breathing, move on to step two.
2. **Move them onto their side, with the upper leg pulled slightly forward and tilt their head back: this is known as the 'Recovery Position'.**

Putting them in this position with their head back helps keep their airway open. It ensures their tongue falls forward and any blood or vomit can drain out.

3. **Call 999 as soon as possible.**

   If you can't call 999, get someone else to do it.

MILD CHOKING

If the airway is only partly blocked, the person will usually be able to speak, cry, cough or breathe.

In situations like this, a person will usually be able to clear the blockage themselves.

Encourage the person to cough to try to clear the blockage.

Ask them to try to spit out the object if it's in their mouth.

Do not put your fingers in their mouth if you can't see the object, as you risk pushing it further down their mouth.

If coughing doesn't work, start back blows.

SEVERE CHOKING

If choking is severe, the person won't be able to speak, cry, cough or breathe and, without help, they'll eventually become unconscious.

To help an adult or child over one year old:

Stand behind the person and slightly to one side. Support their chest with one hand. Lean the person forward so the object blocking their airway will come out of their mouth, rather than moving further down.

Give up to five sharp blows between the person's shoulder blades with the heel of your hand (the heel is between the palm of your hand and your wrist).

Check if the blockage has cleared.

If not, give up to five abdominal thrusts.

Do not give abdominal thrusts to babies under one year old or to pregnant women.

To perform abdominal thrusts on a person who is severely choking and isn't in one of the above groups:

Stand behind the person who is choking.

Place your arms around their waist and bend them well forward.

Clench one fist and place it just above the person's belly button.

Place your other hand on top of your fist and pull sharply inwards and upwards.

Repeat this up to five times.

The aim is to get the obstruction out with each chest thrust, rather than necessarily doing all five.

If the person's airway is still blocked after trying back blows and abdominal thrusts:

Call 999 and ask for an ambulance. Tell the 999 operator that the person is choking.

Continue with the cycles of five back blows and five abdominal thrusts until help arrives.

The person choking should always be seen by a healthcare professional afterwards to check for any injuries or small pieces of the obstruction that remain.

IF A CHILD IS CHOKING

•	If you can see the object, try to remove it. Don't poke blindly or repeatedly with your fingers. You could make things worse by pushing the object further in and making it harder to remove.
	If your child's coughing loudly, encourage them to carry on coughing to bring up what they're choking on and don't leave them.
	If your child's coughing isn't effective (it's silent or they can't breathe in properly), shout for help immediately and decide whether they're still conscious.
•	If your child's still conscious, but they're either not coughing or their coughing isn't effective, use back blows.

Back blows for babies under one year

•	Sit down and lay your baby face down along your thighs, supporting their head with your hand.

	Give up to five sharp back blows with the heel of one hand in the middle of the back between the shoulder blades.

Back blows for children over one year

•	Lay a small child face down on your lap as you would a baby.
•	If this isn't possible, support your child in a forward-leaning position and give five back blows from behind.
If back blows don't relieve the choking and your baby or child is still conscious, give chest thrusts to infants under one year or abdominal thrusts to children over one year.	
This will create an artificial cough, increasing pressure in the chest and helping to dislodge the object.	

Chest thrusts for children under one year

•	Lay your baby face up along the length of your thighs.
•	Find the breastbone and place two fingers in the middle.
•	Give five sharp chest thrusts (pushes), compressing the chest by about a third.

Abdominal thrusts for children over one year

•	Stand or kneel behind your child. Place your arms under the child's arms and around their upper abdomen.
	Clench your fist and place it between the navel and ribs.
•	Grasp this hand with your other hand and pull sharply inwards and upwards.
•	Repeat up to five times.
	Make sure you don't apply pressure to the lower ribcage, as this may cause damage.

Following chest or abdominal thrusts, reassess your child as follows:

•	If the object still isn't dislodged and your child's still conscious, continue the sequence of back blows and either chest or abdominal thrusts.
	Call out or send for help, if you're still on your own.
•	Don't leave the child.
Call 999 if the blockage doesn't come out after trying back blows and either chest or abdominal thrusts. Keep trying this cycle until help arrives.	
Even if the object has come out, get medical help. Part of the object might have been left behind, or your child might have been hurt by the procedure.	

•	If a choking child is, or becomes, unconscious, put them on a firm, flat surface and shout for help.
	Call 999, putting the phone on speakerphone so your hands are free.
•	Don't leave the child at any stage.
•	Open the child's mouth. If the object's clearly visible and you can grasp it easily, remove it.
•	Start CPR – see above CPR for children and infants.

HEAD INJURY

A blow to the head may result in someone having pain or a headache. There may be a bump on their head and they may look pale.

1. **Ask them to rest and apply something cold to the injury – for example, frozen vegetables wrapped in a tea towel.**
   Applying something cold to the injury will reduce external swelling and pain. When a person has a blow to the head, their brain can be shaken inside the skull as well. This may cause a more serious head injury (for example, concussion), which may make them feel sick or drowsy.
2. **Call 999 if they become drowsy, vomit or their condition gets worse.**
   This could be a sign of a serious injury to the head. If you can't call 999, get someone else to do it.

CONCUSSION

What is concussion?

Concussion happens when the brain is shaken inside the skull because of a blow to the head.

A person with concussion tends to be unresponsive for a few seconds to a few minutes. Most people make a full recovery from concussion, but occasionally it becomes more serious.

Call 999 if you think they have concussion.

What are the signs and symptoms of concussion?

A person may have concussion if they:

- are temporarily unresponsive
- are dizzy
- have a headache
- are confused
- feel sick
- have blurred vision
- get more drowsy
- have no memory of what happened.

Drowning – when someone is unable to breathe because their nose or mouth is submerged in any depth of water or liquid:

Take the person out of the water/liquid and check if they are breathing. If they are not breathing, call 999 and start CPR (see above).

FAINTING

If you or someone you are with feels like they are about to faint, lie down, preferably in a position where your head is low and your legs are raised. This will encourage blood flow to your brain.

If it's not possible to lie down, sit with your head between your knees. If you
think someone is about to faint, you should help them lie down or sit with their head between their knees.
If a person faints and doesn't regain consciousness within one or two minutes, put them into the 'recovery position' – move them onto their side with the upper leg pulled slightly forward and tilt their head back.
You should then dial 999, ask for an ambulance and stay with the person until medical help arrives.

Heart Attack: Prop the person up and under no account move them until the ambulance arrives. Give one adult aspirin to chew (this will thin the blood) but only if they are not allergic to aspirin. Call 999.

Overdosing: If the person is found with an empty bottle of pills, keep the bottle for the paramedics. Try to keep the person awake and if they are already asleep wake them up. Call 999.

Poisoning: Do not try to treat them yourself. Call for medical assistance immediately. However, if you think they have taken pills try to wake them up and get them to spit pills out. Put them into the 'recovery position' (see above). Call 999.

Cuts: If the bleeding is excessive, take a clean dressing and press with your fingers until the bleeding stops. Obviously, if it is a very deep or severe cut, stitches may be needed and so best to go to a hospital to have it checked out and treated.

Insect Bites: For a bee sting, extract using tweezers. For a wasp sting, apply vinegar or apple juice. For mosquito bites, it is best to buy a specific product from your chemist.

Foreign body in the eye: Whilst tempting, do not rub the eye. Instead bathe with eye-wash or warm sterilised/boiled water if that's all you have. To remove anything actually in the eye, always use something soft such as a cotton bud.
As a last resort, try pulling the upper lid gently down and over the lower one. This can effectively dislodge persistent foreign bodies.

Nose bleed: Sit the person down with the head well forward. Ask them to breathe through the mouth and pinch the lower part of the nose.

Burns: Immediately immerse the burn under slowly running cold water for at least ten minutes. Dress with a clean, non-fluffy material. If the burns are severe and extensive, go to a hospital for special treatment.

Dislocated Joint: Sit the person down very gently and support the injured part of the body on a cushion. As soon as possible, see a doctor.
Strained Muscle: Apply an ice-bag (or pack of frozen peas!) for thirty minutes and keep the injured limb rested and elevated.

Stocking your Medicine Cupboard

I suggest you always have the following items to hand and please make sure you are not allergic to any of the suggested creams or medicines. It is common for some people to be allergic to penicillin, for example.

- Thermometer
- Plasters and bandages
- Arnica for bruising
- Calendula cream for sores and cuts (Nelsons do a very good one)
- Savlon antiseptic cream
- Optrex for bathing sore eyes
- Paracetamol for pain
- A soothing cream for bites or stings
- Cotton wool and cotton buds
- Sanitary protection and condoms
- Tea-tree oil to bathe in for flu and to gargle with for a sore throat
- Alka-Seltzer for over-indulgence and indigestion

- Kaolin for an upset stomach and diarrhoea
- Rescue herbal remedy from Bach for PMT and any shock to the system.
- Tweezers for stings and splinters
- Antihistamine in case of hay fever or allergic reaction

Tips for going abroad

Make sure your vaccinations are up to date, depending on where you are travelling to. I always made sure that Tania and Peter had a first aid kit on them with plasters, safety pins, antiseptic wipes, antiseptic cream, cough pastilles, anti-histamine and cotton wool.

SOME
DANISH
TRADITIONS.

Chapter 10: Some Danish Traditions

Denmark, where I grew up, has some wonderful and very homely traditions that I enjoyed as a child and now with my own family.

They're not essential things to know when you leave home, of course, but they are fun to do with family and friends, make your home feel very cosy and can make special times of the even more special.

Tania specifically asked me to include them as she thinks a lot of people would love to hear about them. Her best friend is a real fan of the 'Birthday Table'.

1. The Easter Tree

At Easter, we decorate a large branch that looks like a little tree with painted eggs. Some we keep from year to year and some we buy or make. There are many different ways to make the egg decorations for the tree. Try to be as creative as you can and make it look as festive and colourful as possible.

Eggs – example 1:

Buy small chocolate eggs in paper or foil and glue a thin ribbon around the egg using super-glue. Tie in a bow and attach to tree.

Eggs – example 2:

Using chicken or quail eggs, make them hollow by putting a hole at either end and blowing out the contents. Then you can paint them in any colour or style you wish.

To make them hang, tie some thread around the middle of half a matchstick. Put the match through the hole and pull thread tight so that the match is sitting horizontally. Using the thread, tie a loop so it can hang.

Alternatively, pull a needle with double thread through from the top to the bottom and fasten at the bottom with a pearl or bead. Make sure to leave enough thread to hang it up with.

There are so many ways to make your tree look wonderful. Let your imagination run riot!

2. The Marzipan Evening

Before Christmas we have 'The Marzipan Evening', where we all sit around the kitchen table. It's very cosy and lots of fun. I buy lots of good marzipan and everyone makes sweets in lots of different shapes and colours. Some we decorate with melted chocolate (using a 'Bain Marie'). You can be very inventive and use different food colourings. Some of the things we've made in the past include small fruits and vegetables, using green silk for leaves. To store, keep in an airtight tin and put grease-proof paper between the layers.

3. The Birthday Table

Birthdays were always very special when I was a little girl. It wasn't just because of the presents, but because of the way my mother made our 'Birthday Table'. I've done the same for my children and they tell me that it's the most important part of their birthday. It's a lovely treat for a birthday child or adult, everyone is a special birthday child on his or her birthday. I can't tell you how much adults love this birthday treat too.

You have to get out of bed earlier than the birthday child so that everything's done before he or she comes down for breakfast. Make sure that you use a lovely tablecloth or table mats to make it look pretty. Then put some flowers and leaves around the table setting. Decorate the birthday child's (or adult's) chair with flowers and ribbons. Put some candles on the table with the birthday cards and presents. I leave the table like this for the whole day.

Our cat Tigger and our dog Charlie would always wear a ribbon on birthdays, they liked to feel part of it all!

Chapter 11: A Final Word...

I know there seems so much to remember – from the ordinary things, like eating the right foods and putting the washing machine on at the right programme, to not forgetting to blow out the candles, not losing your keys and being ultra-aware of safety when you're out and about.

My grandma and mother taught me so much but I learnt a lot through my own experiences (and mistakes) setting up home. I'm sure it will be the same for you.

You won't take in everything I've suggested, I'm sure, but my hope is that this book will help you feel more confident and able to enjoy your new exciting adventure as you go from home to home.

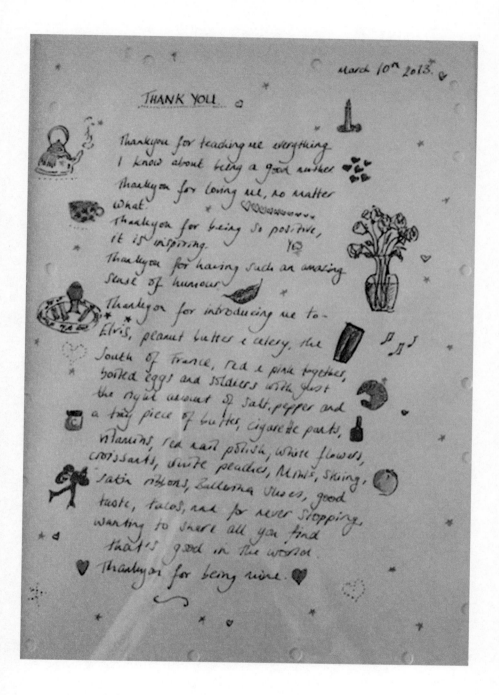

March 10th 2013.

THANK YOU

Thankyou for teaching me everything
I know about being a good mother.
Thankyou for loving me, no matter
what.
Thankyou for being so positive,
it is inspiring.
Thankyou for having such an amazing
sense of humour.
Thankyou for introducing me to-
Elvis, peanut butter & celery, the
South of France, red & pink together,
boiled eggs and soldiers with just
the right amount of salt, pepper and
a tiny piece of butter, cigarette pants,
vitamins, red nail polish, white flowers,
croissants, white peaches, M&M's, skiing,
satin ribbons, ballerina shoes, good
taste, tacos, and for never stopping,
wanting to share all you find
that's good in the world.
Thankyou for being mine.

123